Alabama Studio Style

More Projects, Recipes & Stories Celebrating Sustainable Fashion & Living

For my father, Billy Smith, who taught me to build my life with humility, humanity, and persistence.

Natalie Chanin

Photography by Robert Rausch
Illustrations by Alli Coate
Recipes by Angie Mosier

STC Craft/A Melanie Falick Book
New York

Contents

Introduction   5

CHAPTER 1   **Materials & Tools**   9

CHAPTER 2   **Stitches & Seams**   19

CHAPTER 3   **Garments & Techniques**   31

CHAPTER 4   **Projects & Recipes**   67

Basic Tank Dress   69

String-Quilted Pillow   73

Tank Dress with Relief Appliqué   79

Eyelet-Embroidered Placemats & Napkins   83

Alabama Studio Autumn Brunch   87

Woven Farm Chairs (or Friendship Chairs)   95

Cotton-Jersey Pulls   99

Eyelet-Embroidered Gore Skirt   101

Angie's Fall Scarf   105

Market Bags   107

Medallion Boudoir Pillow   109

Alabama Studio Celebration   112

Inked & Quilted Camisole Dress   119

Circle-Spiral Tunic   123

String-Quilted & Stenciled Tank Top   127

Dinner-on-the-Ground Table   131

Alabama Studio Pickling Party   132

Canning-Jar Covers   137

Eyelet Doily   139

Homemade Cake Plate   143

Small Medallion Placemats   145

Alabama Studio Apron   147

Stenciled & Sewn Table   149

Relief Appliqué Chair Pillow   153

Small Medallion Pillow   155

Spiral Appliqué & Beaded Camisole Dress   157

Angie's Fall Design Variations   163

Acknowledgments   174

About the Author   175

Row 1: Wrap top, Fall/Winter 2002 (photo by Gili Chen); Supply and pattern closet at Lovelace Crossroads; Lovelace Crossroads, exterior view; Dress, Ceremony Collection, Spring/Summer 2009. Row 2: Home Collection, Spring/Summer 2009 (photo by Rinne Allen); Corset, Spring/Summer 2004; Dress, Spring/Summer 2008 (photo by Peter Stanglmayr); Woven Farm Chairs (photo by Elizabeth DeRamus). Row 3: Dress, Spring/Summer 2003; Alabama Chanin Jewelry; Fabric books (photo by Elizabeth DeRamus); Revolution Collection, Fall/Winter 2008.

Introduction

Style. Some are born with it; others cultivate it; and for many of us, it is a slow process of simply growing into who we are. This growth can take a day, a year, a lifetime, or generations. I am reminded of this each time I read this quote by famed American interior designer Sister Parish: "(E)ven the simplest wicker basket can become priceless when it is loved and cared for through the generations of a family."

Customers and journalists often attempt to put a name to the style of products we create at Alabama Chanin. They say, "It does not fit into this style or that trend. It is not primitive. It is not rural. Does it have a name?" In struggling to answer that question, I took a close look at our body of work and how we came to create it and realized how intertwined it is with my personal journey.

Style is not something I was born with, it is something I have developed over the years. I grew up in a community where a framed print purchased at the local furniture store was called art. In fact, hanging over my desk today are two prints from my parents' house: Thomas Lawrence's *Pinkie* and Thomas Gainsborough's *Blue Boy*. I hung them there as a reminder of my roots, and I often jokingly say, "I went to the art school of Pinkie and Blue Boy."

And while that joke has some truth to it, I have come to realize that I was surrounded by art growing up: the art of making something from nothing. Seeds planted in the ground became gourmet family meals. Feed sacks and scraps of fabric became dresses and beautiful quilts that are prized today but back then were considered nothing more than simple, everyday objects. These pieces of art are the core of my visual language, my vernacular, and my community.

It still amazes me that I found my way from Florence, Alabama, to the College of Design at North Carolina State University in Raleigh, where I studied environmental design with an emphasis on textiles. There I melded those scraps of fabric from my childhood with the concise design theories of the Bauhaus masters and my life changed forever. It was the dichotomy of these seemingly disparate influences that fueled my desire to learn, make, and design.

From design school I headed to New York's Seventh Avenue to work in the fashion industry. In New York I learned about product development and production and, eventually, the way that I *did not* want to work. While visiting production facilities, I saw the squalor of an industry that was built on toxic waste and human suffering. And no matter how I tried, I could not find my place in that world. However difficult those lessons, I am grateful today for the experience, as it forced me to examine my values, to question my role, and, finally, it led me across the ocean to work in Europe.

I spent ten wonderful years as a fashion (and sometimes prop) stylist for magazines, advertising, and film. This meant that I devoted hundreds of hours to shopping and doing market research at designer boutiques, thrift stores, flea markets, and bookstores. I often call this time my "graduate school." It gave me the opportunity to meld the lessons I learned in my childhood, at design school, and during my time in the fashion industry, and apply them to color, texture, shape, garments, photography, film, imagery, and storytelling. It was during this period that I became the designer, and the person, I am today.

In my first book, *Alabama Stitch Book*, I shared the story of how a small decision in the year 2000 to cut apart a T-shirt and hand-stitch it back together led me home to Florence to work with the stitchers and quilters of my community to produce a collection of one-of-a-kind T-shirts, along with a documentary film about old-time quilting circles, and then to found Alabama Chanin. In *Alabama Stitch Book*, I introduced the stitching, stenciling, beading techniques, and designs with which we began.

When I deconstructed that first T-shirt, I had no idea it would lead me to discover my true calling as a designer building a fashion and lifestyle company committed to what today is called Slow Design. The term *Slow Design* grew out of the Slow Food Movement and is defined by the process of building a product and a company on handcraft, commitment to community, and respect for the environment. Good, clean, fair—that is the motto.

Funnily, almost the day *Alabama Stitch Book* hit bookstore shelves, we moved our offices from the "country" to the "city." After seven years of living, working, laughing, sewing, and growing in our house at Lovelace Crossroads, in a home built by my father's father, next to one built by my mother's father, we moved past "The Crossroads" and on to "The Factory."

I am a creature of habit and was reluctant to leave our rural roots for a more industrial space, but the studio at The Factory has truly become our home. From this new studio and new perspective, our once-simple exploration has emerged into a multidisciplinary creative platform for collaborations, special projects and events, and many ideas. *Alabama Studio Style* reflects these next steps in our journey.

Here I share more techniques and projects, for both clothing and home décor, plus three menus with recipes that I developed with Southern food expert Angie Mosier. It is my belief that by sharing the basics of life—food, clothing, and shelter—we are all connected. Through design and production of beautiful, lasting, and soulful products, we are providing the platform for our families and greater communities to live truly rich, healthy, and meaningful lives. And it is this connection between making and beauty that I have set out to share in this book.

While *Alabama Stitch Book* and *Alabama Studio Style* can be used independently, each introduces different techniques that can be easily mixed and matched. It is my hope that these rich and varied techniques, stories, and recipes will inspire you to create, sew, and cook while developing your own stories, your own voice, and your own style.

This journey to Alabama Chanin—and to my own voice—has been a lovely one. It has been filled with colors, textures, shapes, and explorations. And these explorations are what continue to thrill me today. The journey has motivated me to care about my environment in all ways, the way I produce and manufacture goods, grow and prepare my food, decorate my living room, and participate in my family and community. The path has been filled with ups and downs, twists, turns, growing, learning, laughing, taking in, and, of course, letting go. It is a story painted with fabric, shaped by hands, held tight with threads and people.

Alabama Studio Style is at the core of Alabama Chanin. It is my home, my work, my love, my people. It is a way of looking at the world that, consequently, defines how the world looks. It is food, clothing, and shelter sewn together into a harmonious pattern that enriches our lives every day.

Chapter 1
Materials & Tools

At Alabama Chanin, we're committed to using ecologically sustainable materials and tools for every stage of our work. We stitch together recycled cotton T-shirts with organically grown cotton-jersey yardage to make couture garments and home furnishings. We sew and weave our fabric scraps and yarns to create chair seats and to add decorative elements to vintage furniture. We combine welded metal scraps with sticks we find in the woods to make chandeliers and sculpture.

It's this playful use of materials that inspires us and creates a nest of surfaces and textures that make us feel at home—in our clothing, in our living rooms, and at our kitchen tables.

This chapter offers an overview of the materials and tools that we use daily and are needed for the projects in this book. Most are available at fabric and craft stores and from our online store at www.alabamachanin.com. We don't recommend purchasing everything right away but rather building your toolkits slowly along with your skills and interests.

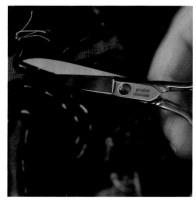

Cotton Jersey

Cotton jersey has been at the center of our work since I cut up the very first T-shirt and sewed it back together again in 2000. While I still love to work with recycled T-shirts and incorporate them into our work every chance I get, I now also design with new cotton-jersey yardage. The certified organic fiber that our cotton-jersey yardage is made from is grown in Texas and spun in Tennessee; the fabric is knit in South Carolina, dyed in Mississippi and North Carolina, and then sent to us to cut apart and sew back together into an array of products. Unlike working with recycled T-shirts, using cotton-jersey yardage allows us to work with larger pattern pieces, like those for the Camisole and Tank Dresses in this book, without having to break up a pattern into T-shirt-sized sections—18 for the dresses in question—and then seam the numerous sections back together again. Starting to work with fabric yardage was very freeing for me as a designer since it allowed me to think about the structure of a garment solely from the perspective of fit. And, finally, using yardage has allowed us to provide a more consistent product when producing larger projects and orders.

We still strongly believe in working with recycled cotton-jersey T-shirts as often as possible. But we've realized that sometimes it's more environmentally sound to work with new, organic cotton-jersey yardage that's grown and manufactured not far from our own door rather than shipping in recycled T-shirts and running dye vat after dye vat to get the number of shirts we need in the desired colors. Over the years, I've learned that every step of the process must be considered to find the path of least environmental harm. This remains the philosophy that we strive to follow daily.

Understanding Cotton-Jersey Yardage

Because T-shirts are such a staple of modern dressing, both fabric and garment manufacturers are always trying to introduce new weights, finishes, and other appealing and differentiating options into their lines. As a result, the language of cotton jersey can be confusing and sometimes overwhelming. Following is the basic information that you need to know to work on the projects in this book.

Cotton-jersey fabric is typically knit in a tube. It is either sold in tubular form, often 30" wide, or it can be split and spread open, then sold flat like most other fabric. Manufacturers knit cotton jersey in a variety of widths but the most commonly available split and spread-open fabric is 60" wide. For this reason, most of the projects in this book require very little yardage, and some of them can be made using remnants and scraps.

I always choose a sturdy medium- to heavyweight cotton jersey since I find this weight easier to sew and more durable than lightweight jersey, which can pill or tear. When considering whether to buy a particular cotton-jersey fabric, I hold it in my hands and ask myself if it feels appropriate for my project and then make my decision based on what my hands tell me. Although there's a technical term for what I'm assessing—it is the fabric's *hand*—my decision tends to be based on my initial gut reaction.

We wash all of our cotton jersey before cutting in order to preshrink it, which I highly recommend you do before embarking on a project. Washing before sewing ensures that your finished project will not shrink after completion.

Finding the Grain Line

Before cutting your fabric, you'll need to find the fabric's grain line so that you can match it with the pattern's marked grain line and hence cut out your project correctly. Cutting a garment's pattern pieces correctly—with the fabric's and pattern's grain lines matched—enhances the finished garment's stretchability at key points (like the armholes) and, in turn, your comfort while wearing the garment.

In a knit fabric, the term *grain line* refers to the direction of the stitches making up the fabric, which, in the case of cotton jersey, typically run vertically along the fabric's length. If you look closely at cotton jersey's right side, you'll see straight vertical columns of stitches that make up the grain line. On cotton jersey's wrong side, you'll see a series of little loops. To cut with the grain of the fabric, align your scissors or rotary cutter with the fabric's grain, that is, its vertical columns of stitches.

Right Side

Wrong Side

Thread

There are many types of thread available, and it's important to choose wisely. For most sewing, we like to use what is called button craft thread (also known as buttonhole, carpet, and craft thread), which is thicker than ordinary sewing thread and comes in about 10 colors. Typically made with a polyester core surrounded by cotton, button craft thread is one of the strongest threads available. You can wash it again and again without it breaking or wearing, and its polished finish helps prevent it from weakening as you endlessly pull it through your fabric while sewing a project. Its thickness is also ideal for embroidered embellishment.

In addition to button craft thread for general construction sewing, we use a standard all-purpose thread for basting necklines and armholes before constructing garments to keep these curved edges from stretching.

We also use embroidery floss, a thread composed of six loosely twisted strands, for some of our techniques, such as backstitched reverse appliqué (see page 54). We never use this floss for sewing seams since the strands will not withstand the stress that garment seams are subjected to. Embroidery floss is sold in a seemingly unlimited variety of colors, often in small skeins, at most fabric and craft stores.

Understanding and "Loving" Your Thread

When thread is made, microscopic, squiggly cotton fibers are combed in the same direction into two strands, each called a ply. Then one of these plies is twisted to the right (in an "S" twist), while the other strand is twisted to the left (in a "Z" twist). The two plies are finally twisted around each other as tightly as possible, so that, when released, they relax, "expand," and join around one another to create a single strand of thread. The tension between the two plies explains why thread doesn't fray and also why it sometimes knots as you sew with it. The knotting is caused by excess tension. But there is a way of reducing this tension, a ritual I call "loving" your thread.

To love your thread, cut a piece twice as long as the distance from your fingers to your elbow. Thread your needle, pulling the thread through the needle until the two ends of the thread are the same length. Hold the doubled thread between your thumb and index finger, and run your fingers along it from the needle to the end of the loose tails. Repeat several times. What you're doing is working the tension out of the high-strung thread with rubbing, pressure, and the natural oils on your fingers. In the process, you've also taken a moment to calm the tension in your mind and add just a little bit of love to your project. Now you're ready to tie off your knot (see page 21) and start sewing.

Alabama Studio Style Toolkits

I've always loved tool stores—whether my local hardware, fabric, or kitchen supply shop. I delight in scouring flea markets and secondhand venues for tools that are both useful and beautifully designed. Below you'll find recommendations for starting, keeping, and expanding your own toolkits for cutting, marking, stitching, and stenciling. These are the tools we use on a daily basis at Alabama Chanin.

Cutting Tools

• Garment scissors, for cutting fabric for large projects

• 4" embroidery scissors, for small, detailed work and cutting thread

• 5" knife-edge sewing and craft scissors, for making longer cuts and trimming fabric

• Paper scissors, for cutting out paper patterns

• Seam ripper

• Rotary cutter

• Cutting mat

• Craft knife

Marking Tools

• 6" transparent, gridded, flexible plastic ruler, for drawing designs and stitching lines

• 18" transparent plastic ruler, for making patterns and cutting fabric with a rotary cutter

• Tailor's chalk

• Disappearing-ink fabric pens, for small tasks like marking patterns, transferring stencils in small areas, drawing shapes for cutting out appliqués (always test the pen on a discreet spot on your fabric before using it)

• Pattern paper (lightweight paper with a grid of dots on one side; available at fabric stores) or butcher paper (white paper waxed on one side; available at grocery stores), for masking off areas of a stencil, protecting work surfaces, and making patterns (both types of paper will work for all of these purposes, but butcher paper is cheaper and better for stenciling; pattern paper is better for patterns)

Stitching Tools

• Sewing needle (I prefer a #9 sharp needle)

• Beading needle (I prefer a #10 large-eyed millinery needle, which accommodates thick button craft thread but is still able to pass through many beads)

• Thimble, to protect fingertips while sewing

• A small rubber finger cap (sold at office supply stores), to get a grip on a needle

• Needle-nose pliers, to help pull a needle through many layers of fabric

• Straight pins (I find white glass-topped pins easier to grab than standard pins)

Stenciling Tools

• Medium- or heavyweight transparent film (usually Mylar, available at craft stores), for making stencils

• Acrylic pennant felt, for making stencils

• Spray adhesive, to hold a stencil in place while painting it

• Permanent or textile markers, for transferring stencil designs to fabric (avoid red, which bleeds in the wash)

• Textile paint, for transferring a stencil design onto fabric

• Clean spray bottles with adjustable nozzles, to spray textile paint onto fabric

• Stencil brushes, for transferring textile paint to fabric (we use both large, natural-bristle brushes and sponge brushes; any clean household sponge will also work)

• Butcher paper (see Marking Tools on page 14; used additionally, waxed side down, between the front and back of a T-shirt to keep paint from bleeding through the stencil onto the fabric)

• Airbrush gun and air compressor, recommended only if/when you get very serious about spray-painting stencil designs onto fabric and other surfaces (see page 45)

Ironing

Ironing is an integral part of our sewing process. We use it to press seams for felling (see page 28), to press our relief appliqué (see page 53), and generally to finish garments. Here are a few tips:

Start with excellent tools. For the projects in this book, you'll need a high-quality iron and an ironing board. You may also want to invest in a tailor's ham and sleeve board for more elaborate construction projects. However, in a pinch, a rolled-up towel can fill in for a sleeve board. You'll also need a spray bottle able to produce a fine mist to dampen fabric.

Test fabric. We use the cotton setting for all of our ironing because we always work with cotton jersey. For best results, test a swatch of every fabric before you start ironing. If your iron seems to stick or pull on the fabric, your heat setting is probably too high. Note that we do not iron our cotton jersey before cutting a project because ironing can stretch the fabric, causing the cut pieces to skew.

Iron damp fabric. Ironing damp fabric helps to remove any set-in wrinkles. Iron clothes, especially those made of cotton, rayon, and silk, while they are still damp by removing them from the dryer before they are completely dry. If that's not convenient, dampen dried clothes with a steam iron or sprinkle them with warm water. Allow the moisture to permeate the fabric.

Enhance contours. Garments like our dresses have shaped waistlines, princess seams, and armholes so that they will curve around the body in a flattering way. While constructing a project and when it is finished, use the iron to enhance those intended contours.

Prevent wrinkles. There is an old saying, "Cool remembers; warm forgets." Put this into practice while you work by allowing your fabric to cool and dry before moving it (if you don't wait these few seconds, you may actually create more wrinkles). Once the fabric is cool, move the freshly ironed surface away from you; this keeps your body from coming in contact with the fabric and making more wrinkles.

Iron both sides of double-layer items. For an item made with two layers of fabric, iron it on the wrong side first and then on the right side to help it better retain its shape. For an item made with one layer of fabric, either side can be ironed first.

Take care around embroidery and beading. Iron your embroidery work facedown on a thick towel to help it retain its shape and dimension. Iron pieces with beading on their wrong side so that the iron does not come in direct contact with the beads.

Chapter 2
Stitches & Seams

While the stitches that we use at Alabama Chanin are age-old, our goal is always to use them in new ways to create garments, furnishings, and fabrics that feel contemporary. This chapter presents an overview of the stitches we used to complete the projects in this book.

Learning to Stitch

Although much of my working life revolves around sewing, I nearly failed my first home economics class in high school. I remember my teacher admonishing me that I would "never be able to sew." Her remarks about my machine-sewing skills were justly deserved since my pale yellow apron was a cockeyed approximation of a rectangle. Today, I prefer to sew by hand and have been awed and inspired by the hand-sewing and embroidery talents of our local artisans.

If you're new to sewing, there are a few simple tips to keep in mind, all of which are explained here. Then all you'll need is a little practice to build your skills.

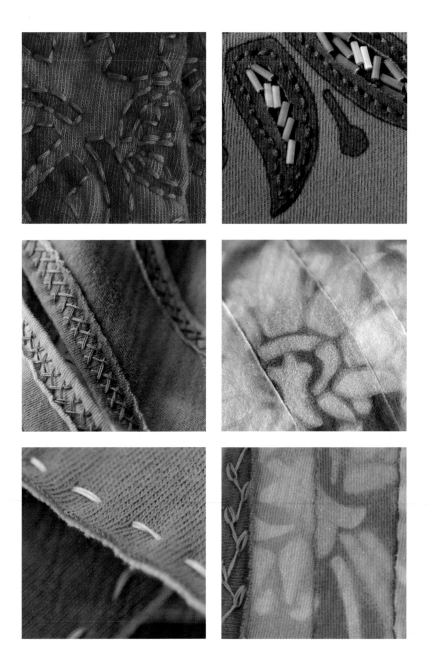

Chalking Your Stitching Line

Chalking a stitching line gives you an easy, straight guideline to follow as you stitch. To chalk a stitching line, simply use tailor's chalk and a small ruler to mark your seam lines with a dashed line $\frac{1}{4}$" from the edge.

Chalking Your Stitching Line

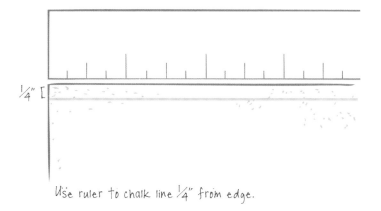

Use ruler to chalk line $\frac{1}{4}$" from edge.

Stitch Length

For the projects in this book, you'll be stitching with a doubled length of thread. Your stitches should be between $\frac{1}{8}$" and $\frac{1}{4}$" long, with the spaces between the stitches the same length as the stitches themselves. Aim for uniform stitches and spaces in between.

Stitching with Even Tension

In hand-sewing, the tension is key since it determines how tightly or loosely your stitches lie on the fabric. If your tension is too tight—that is, if you pull your thread too tight as you sew through the fabric—your seam will likewise be pulled too tight and will start to gather up. If your tension is too loose, your seam will be too loose and will buckle.

You can control tension by using your fingers to guide the stitches. After completing each pull of your needle, check your tension to make sure that your fabric lies flat, smooth, and even. Adjust the tension of the stitches you've sewn by holding on to both sides of your project and giving a gentle pull or two in opposite directions to make the fabric lie perfectly flat. You can also place your thumb on the bottom of your project fabric and your index finger on the top and gently rub that thread in the direction of your stitches to get the perfect tension. Once you get into a stitching rhythm, this maneuver will become second nature.

Knotting Off

In hand-sewing, your knot holds your entire seam. Since cotton jersey is a knit fabric made by looping small threads through one another to form a knitted "web," very small holes are formed where the thread loops. If you knot your thread with a small knot, that knot can pull through any of these small holes and may also break one of the knit fabric's tiny threads, causing the fabric to "run" and produce an even bigger hole. That's why, in most of our projects, we tell you to double your thread and use a large double knot to anchor the thread.

Another way to ensure durability is to leave a long, ½" tail of thread after you tie off each knot. Wearing and washing your garment over time will cause these thread tails to become shorter and shorter, potentially wearing down to about ¼". For this reason, if you start with long tails, you can ensure that the garment maintains its original integrity from the first day it was knotted. We like to say that we leave long tails so that our garments will remain intact for this generation and the next and the next.

One important decision we make when starting any project is how to handle the knots. There are two options: knots that show on the right (public) side of the projects and knots that show on the wrong side. Either of these knots can be used throughout an entire project or combined with the other type.

Tying a Double Knot

Second knot being formed

First knot

Cut ½" from knot

Double knot completed

Make loop with your needle; then pull needle through loop, using your forefinger or thumb to nudge knot into place so that it's flush with fabric. Then repeat this process a second time to make double knot. After making second knot, cut thread, leaving ½" tail.

The Stitches

We use two basic types of stitches in our work: stitches that don't stretch, for construction and reverse appliqué, and stitches that do stretch, for necklines, armholes, and other areas in a project that require "give."

Basic Non-Stretch Stitches

Straight (or Running) Stitch This is the most basic stitch of all and is used in this book for both general construction and for embellishing a fabric with appliqué, reverse appliqué, and beading. To make this stitch, work from right to left (or vice versa if you're left-handed), as shown in the drawing below, and make both your stitches and the spaces between them between ⅛" and ¼" in length. Your stitching should look the same on the front and back of the fabric.

Straight (or Running) Stitch

Bring needle from back of fabric at A, go back down at B, and come out at C, making stitches and spaces between them the same length.

Basting Stitch A basting stitch is just a looser, longer version of the straight stitch, and is used to temporarily hold, or baste, layers of fabric together as you construct or embellish your project. A basting stitch also helps preserve the shape of the cut fabric and prevent a cut edge, like a curved neckline or armhole, from stretching as you work.

Use a single strand of all-purpose thread to sew simple basting stitches. There's no need to knot the thread at the beginning or end of a line of basting stitches since you want to be able to remove these stitches easily once they're no longer needed. Keep your stitches consistently about ½" long, and make the spaces between them about the same length.

Basting Stitch

Make both stitches and spaces between them about ½" long.

Backstitch The backstitch is another variation of the straight stitch, which fills in the entire stitching line with thread and looks very much like machine stitching. The backstitch is easy to learn, even though it may seem confusing at first to work "backwards" in order to move forward. This is a durable stitch for any project and is especially good for outlining a shape or an area of your work.

Backstitch

Bring needle up at A, go back down at B, and exit at C.

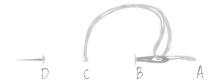

Then insert needle just ahead of B and come up at D.

Insert needle just ahead of C, and come up at E. Continue this overall pattern.

Blanket Stitch A blanket stitch is traditionally used to work a border around the outside edge of a blanket. At Alabama Chanin, we use the blanket stitch to work around a central point to make our eyelets on page 62 and also to stabilize the edges of our refurbished quilts (see Textile Stories on page 161). Generally, we use a doubled strand of button craft thread for this stitch, but sometimes we use embroidery floss in areas where a project will not get a lot of wear.

Blanket Stitch

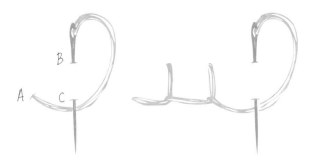

Bring your needle up at A, hold thread with your finger to right of where it emerged. Then insert needle at B, about 1/4" to right of A and 1/4" above it, and stitch back out at C, directly below B, making sure needle stitches over, not under, thread. Pull thread out so that it lies tightly against thread at C, and repeat process. Continue working this stitch, keeping its length and spacing consistent, until you've completed entire edge or eyelet.

Basic Stretch Stitches

Because cotton-jersey fabric stretches, sewing a cotton-jersey garment requires using a stretch stitch for areas that likewise need to be able to stretch, such as a neckline or armhole. In addition to providing the necessary "give" to a seam, each of these stretch stitches is also decorative. Other stretch stitches you might want to try include the zigzag, cross, zigzag coral, chevron, arrowhead, Cretan, snail trail, and feather stitch, whose directions can all easily be found in most embroidery-stitch guides.

Work all of the stitches shown here from left to right (or vice versa if you're left-handed) along a pair of imaginary parallel lines, as shown in the drawings.

Herringbone Stitch This is one of my favorite stitches. It is easy to master and works up quickly.

Herringbone Stitch

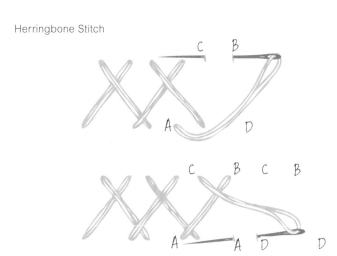

Bring needle up at A, insert it down at B, bring it back up again at C, and insert it down at D to complete one herringbone stitch. To start next stitch, come back up again at new A, stitch back down at new B, and continue working in above pattern to create row of herringbone stitches, keeping their length and spacing consistent.

Parallel Whipstitch The parallel whipstitch is, hands-down, the best stitch for appliqué because it attaches the appliqué very securely to the base fabric. At Alabama Chanin, we also use the parallel whipstitch for neckline binding; for open-felling seams (see page 29), as in the Basic Tank Dress on page 69; and for decorative embroidery for attaching beaded borders.

Parallel Whipstitch

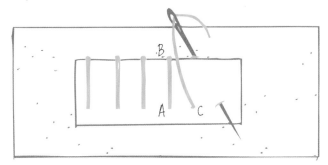

Come up at A, go back down at B, and come up again at C, making stitches and spaces between them both ⅜". Repeat this pattern along length of edge to be whipstitched or to stitch applique to background fabric.

Rosebud Stitch Traditionally called a chained feather, this stitch is a simple variation of the feather stitch. We dubbed it the rosebud stitch because it looks like there are tiny rose buds growing from each "stem." I originally used this stitch on my Fall/Winter 2006 Rose Collection, inspired by my great-grandmother Llewellyn's love of roses.

Rosebud Stitch

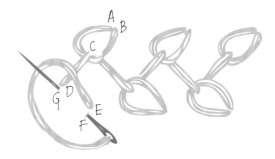

Work this stitch along two imaginary parallel lines, starting by bringing needle up at A. Loop thread below and to right of A, and insert needle back down at B, just to right of A. Bring needle back up at C, pulling thread over, not under, thread loop you made. Insert needle back down at D, and come up at E. Loop thread below and to left of E, insert needle at F, and come up G, pulling thread over, not under, thread loop. Continue this stitching pattern, alternating back and forth between parallel lines to form zigzag rosebud stitch.

Seams

At Alabama Chanin, we pride ourselves on our very strong hand-stitched seams, whose strength rivals that of machine-stitched seams because of the sturdy button craft thread (see page 12) with which we stitch them.

Each season we make basic design decisions about the placement of seams on each garment in the collection. First we decide if we want the seams to be visible on the garment's right side, which tends to highlight its structure, or hidden on the wrong side, which tends to highlight the embellishment of the fabric. Next we decide if we want the seams to be floating or felled. Floating seams give a rough, deconstructed look. Felled seams lie flat and are stronger, thanks to the extra line of stitches that the felling requires.

As a general rule, all of our seams are ¼" wide (that is, we stitch the seam line ¼" from the fabric's cut raw edge). If a different seam width is called for in a given project, the directions will tell you.

The seams shown on the garments at right are (left to right): felled on the wrong side, felled on the right side, and open-felled with parallel whipstitch.

Floating Seams

A floating seam is a regular seam whose seam allowances are left untouched after the seam is sewn. They are allowed to "float" rather than being stitched down.

Floating Seam

When using floating seams in a project, it's important to make sure that every seam floats, even if it's intersected by another seam. To stitch a floating seam that intersects another floating seam, stitch under the sewn seam being intersected so that its allowances remain floating, and then begin stitching again as usual on the seam you're sewing.

Intersecting Floating Seams

Floating Seam on Right Side To make a floating seam that shows on the right side of a garment or project, pin the two cut fabrics being seamed with their wrong sides together, then stitch the seam on the right side of the fabric. The resulting seam is visible on the project's right side.

Floating Seam on Right Side

Floating Seam on Wrong Side To make a floating seam that is hidden on the right side of a garment or project, pin the two cut fabrics being seamed with their right sides together; then stitch the seam on the wrong side of the fabric. The resulting seam is only visible on the project's wrong side.

Floating Seam on Wrong Side

Felled Seams

On our felled seam, the cut edges of the seam allowances still show, but, unlike on a floating seam, these allowances are sewn down with a row of stitches parallel to the seam line.

To sew a felled seam, work a regular floating seam; then fold that seam's allowances over together to one side, and stitch them down flat to the project with a second row of stitches parallel to the seam line.

To decide which direction to fell your seams, start at the center front or center back of your garment, and always fell seams toward the side of your body. As a general rule, side seams should be felled toward your back.

Felled Seam on Right Side To sew a felled seam on the right side of a garment or project, start by sewing a floating seam on the right side (see above right). Then fold the finished seam's allowances over together to one side, and stitch them down on the right side of the project with a row of parallel stitches $\frac{1}{8}$" from the allowances' cut edges or down the center of the seam allowances. The resulting seam will be visible on the right side of the project.

Felled Seam on Right Side

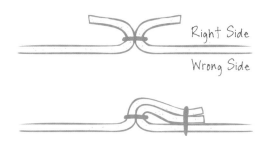

Felled Seam on Wrong Side To sew a felled seam on the wrong side of a garment or project, start by sewing a floating seam on the wrong side. Then fold the finished seam's allowances over together to one side, and stitch them down on the wrong side of the project with a row of parallel stitches $\frac{1}{8}$" from the allowances' cut edges or down the center of the seam allowances. The resulting seam will be invisible on the right side of the project.

Felled Seam on Wrong Side

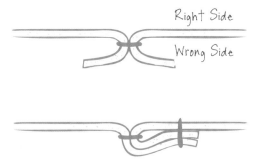

Open-Felled Seam We sew a variation on our felled seam that we call an open-felled seam, which involves opening up the seam's allowances and sewing each one down to the base fabric with a row of stitches parallel to the seam. The resulting seam has a parallel stitching line on each side of the seam line itself.

To sew an open-felled seam on the right side of a garment or project, start by sewing a floating seam on the right side. Then open up the finished seam's allowances to each side, and stitch them down on the right side of the project with a row of stitches $\frac{1}{8}$" from each allowance's cut edge and parallel to it or down the center of each seam allowance. The resulting open-felled seam will be visible on the right side of the project. To open-fell a seam on the wrong side, start by sewing a floating seam on the wrong side, and then proceed as above for sewing an open-felled seam on the right side. We often use an embroidery stitch for felling these open-felled seams, rather than the traditional straight stitch (see the Basic Tank Dress on page 69)

Open-Felled Seam

Wrap-Stitching Seams

To anchor your seam and ensure that it stays flat with no hint of gathering or pulling, begin and end it with what we call "wrap-stitching" the fabric's raw edges. To do this, wrap a loop of thread around the edge of the fabric at the first and last stitches, as shown in the drawing below.

Wrap-Stitching Seams

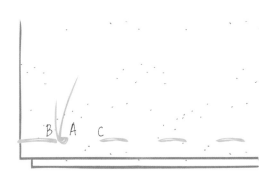

To start your seam, make a double knot and insert needle at A. Wrap thread around side of fabric to front, go back in at B (right next to A), then come up at C, and stitch seam. Wrap again before knotting off at the end of the seam.

CHAPTER 3
Garments & Techniques

From cutting our couture garments to sewing each seam and weaving each chair seat, every piece produced at Alabama Chanin is made by hand. In *Alabama Stitch Book*, we presented our signature techniques: stenciling, reverse appliqué, and appliqué. In this book, we present variations of these techniques and also some new techniques that we've used to expand our collections. I thrive on mixing and matching these treatments for variety in our projects and find inspiration in the endless possibilities.

Note: For projects in this book, the Angie's Fall stencil artwork (shown here) was enlarged by 325 percent.
This artwork can be photocopied and enlarged from this page or it can be downloaded full-size from www.alabamachanin.com.

Garment Patterns

The master pattern for all the projects in this book is the Camisole Dress pattern show below, as it is laid out on the pattern sheet at the back of the book. This pattern can be used to make the Camisole Dress and four variations—the Camisole Tunic, Tank Dress,

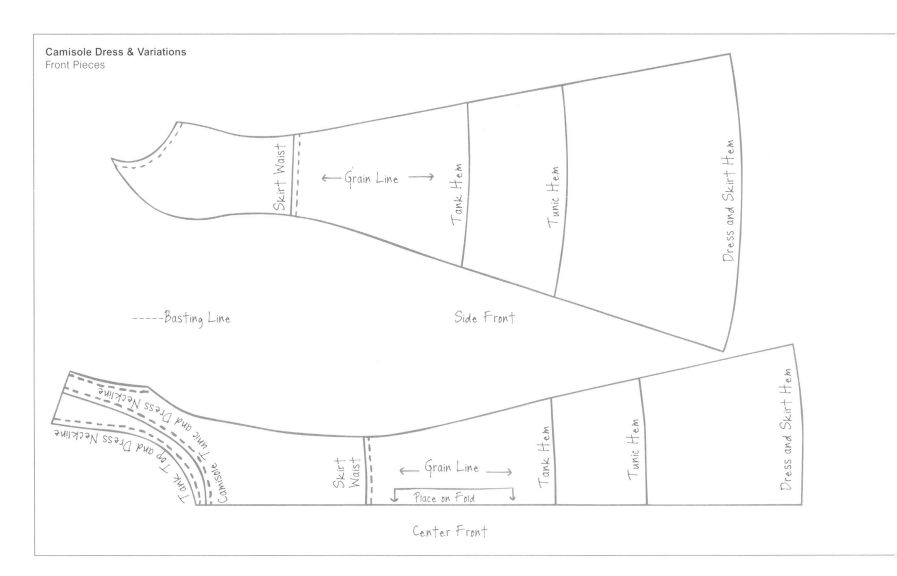

Camisole Dress & Variations
Front Pieces

Skirt Waist

← Grain Line →

Tank Hem

Tunic Hem

Dress and Skirt Hem

-----Basting Line

Side Front

Tank Top and Dress Neckline

Tunic and Dress Neckline

Camisole

Skirt Waist

← Grain Line →

Place on Fold

Tank Hem

Tunic Hem

Dress and Skirt Hem

Center Front

Tank Top, and Gore Skirt—which are all featured in the book's projects and described on the following pages. This pattern can also be used to make two more variations, a Camisole Top and a Tank Tunic, which are not among the book's projects.

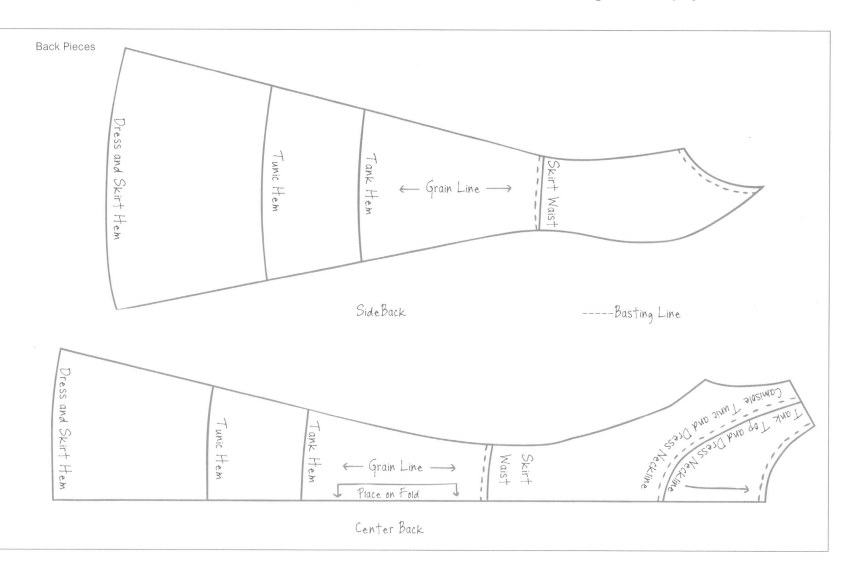

Back Pieces

Dress and Skirt Hem

Tunic Hem

Tank Hem

← Grain Line →

Skirt Waist

Side Back

-----Basting Line

Dress and Skirt Hem

Tunic Hem

Tank Hem

← Grain Line →

↓ Place on Fold ↓

Skirt Waist

Camisole Tunic and Dress Neckline

Tank Top and Dress Neckline

Center Back

Camisole Dress This dress has thin straps, a revealing neckline, and scooped-out back. It is nipped in at the waist and curve of the back to flatter the figure. You'll find that the fitted bust and waist provide support, but the stretchable cotton-jersey fabric molds itself to each person who wears it, whatever her proportions. The six-gore skirt flares from the waist to accommodate any hip size.

Camisole Tunic This tunic is a shortened version of the Camisole Dress. It is approximately 28" long from the shoulder but can be easily shortened or lengthened.

Camisole Variations

Top Hem

Tunic Hem

Dress Hem

Tank Dress This dress has a raised front and back neckline and a wider shoulder strap than the Camisole Dress (see left).

Tank Top This top has a raised front and back neckline, and a wider strap at the shoulder, and its length is approximately 23" from the shoulder. This length can be easily shortened or lengthened at the bottom edge.

Gore Skirt To make this six-gore, flared, pull-on skirt, we simply cut the Camisole Dress off at the waistline. Then we add a fold-over elastic waistband sewn with a stretch stitch (see page 24).

Fold-Over Elastic Waistband

Fold-over elastic, which comes in many beautiful colors, is knitted with a ridge down the center that allows it to easily fold in half lengthwise. To use it to create a waistband for the Gore Skirt, simply slip the edge of your fabric as deep into the fold of the elastic as you can and then stitch the elastic down using a stretchable stitch (see page 24).

Tank Variations

Top Hem

Tunic Hem

Dress Hem

Gore Skirt

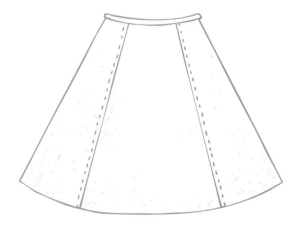

Cutting Out a Pattern

Whether you work with a ready-made pattern or make your own, cutting out the pattern is important and requires precision since the pattern is the foundation of your project. Below are instructions for cutting out a pattern using cotton-jersey yardage (see page 10).

Supplies

Project pattern

Cotton-jersey fabric

Tailor's chalk or disappearing-ink fabric pen

Paper scissors

Garment scissors

1. Choose Size and Cut Out Pattern

The garment patterns at the back of this book provide five sizes (from XS to XL) in which the garment can be made. Decide which size garment you want to make (see the guidelines opposite), photocopy or trace the pattern, and use your paper scissors to cut out the photocopied or traced pattern in your desired size.

2. Prepare Fabric for Cutting and Stitching

It's important to prevent the cotton-jersey fabric from stretching as you cut and work with it. To do this, when laying the cotton jersey on your work surface, don't stretch it or smooth it out by pulling on it. Instead, pat it lightly into place with your fingertips. The directions for each project will tell you whether to lay out and cut your fabric single- or double-layer.

3. Transfer Pattern to Fabric

Lay your paper pattern pieces on top of your fabric, making sure the pattern's marked grain line runs in the same direction as the fabric's grain line (see page 11). This is important because, for example, when cutting out a camisole, you want the grain line on the cut fabric pieces to run vertically from the neckline to waistline, so the fabric can stretch around your body. Matching up the pattern's and fabric's grain lines ensures that you're cutting out the pattern piece correctly.

As you trace around your pattern piece with tailor's chalk or a fabric pen, hold the pattern in place with the palm of your hand (or with pattern weights or even canned goods). We prefer holding or weighting the pattern to pinning it on the fabric, which, in the case of cotton jersey, often skews the fabric and makes the cutting uneven. We've also found that this strategy prevents nicking and tearing the pattern, which often results from pinning.

Since many of the projects in this book have more than one pattern piece, we suggest cutting out all the pieces at once. Laying out all the pattern pieces together on your fabric before you start cutting enables you to figure out how to use your fabric most efficiently.

4. Cut Pattern from Fabric

Using garment scissors, cut out the pattern pieces as called for in your project directions, trying your best to cut just inside the chalked line you traced around the pattern. By cutting away all the visible chalk (but not cutting beyond the chalked line), you'll help ensure a perfect fit.

Finding Your Size

When it comes to picking a size, everyone has a personal preference. At Alabama Chanin, we recommend a slightly snug fit to start because, over the course of several wearings and washings, the cotton jersey will relax and begin to take on the body's shape. However, we make an exception when helping people choose a size for garments heavily embellished with decorative stitching and beading since the embellishment tends to limit the cotton jersey's ability to stretch; in this case, we suggest choosing one size larger than your regular dress size. Whatever your fit preference, look at the size chart below to see our general measurements for each pattern size (note that only chest and waist measurements are given since the base pattern's flared, six-gore skirt accommodates a wide range of hip sizes).

One way to ensure that your garment will fit you perfectly is to first make a simple, unembellished version, try it on for size, and then adapt your next garment accordingly. We call these unadorned garments our basics, and we've grown to love them as much as our more elaborate pieces.

	XS	S	M	L	XL
Size	0–2	4–6	6–8	10–12	14–16
Chest	28–30	30–32	32–34	36–38	40–42
Waist	23–24	25–26	27–28	30–32	33–35

Alabama Studio Style Stencils

Stenciling is at the core of all of our collections; it is the sole means by which we transfer decorative patterns onto our fabric. The simplest way to work is to buy a ready-made stencil; they are commonly sold at craft and art supply stores. You can also use existing artwork (either from a book or CD of stencil designs or another source), or make your own stencil. For the projects in this book, we have provided three stencil patterns: Angie's Fall in one size and Medallion in a small and large size. The Small Medallion stencil is provided as a pullout located between pages 144 and 145 and is ready to use. The artwork for the Large Medallion is on page 66; we have enlarged this artwork 335% to create the stencil for all of the projects using the Large Medallion in this book. The artwork for Angie's Fall is on page 31; this artwork has been enlarged 325% to create stencils for all of the projects in this book. If you prefer, you can download the full-size artwork from www.alabamachanin.com.

Making a Stencil

Below are instructions for making a stencil from the artwork in this book or from any other source.

Supplies

Stencil image of your choice

Transparent film, pennant felt, or material of your choice slightly larger than desired size of stencil image

Spray adhesive

Craft knife with sharp blade (sharpness is key to a precise cut)

Cutting mat

Computer with scanning capability or copy machine (optional)

Tools for your choice of stencil-transfer method (see page 42)

1. Choose and Copy Stencil Design

To create a stencil design, you need a stencil image and a method for transferring the image to the surface you want to decorate.

The first step is to photocopy your image if it's printed or if it's on a CD or scanned into your computer, to enlarge or reduce the image to the size you want, and then print it out. If you want the image to be larger than the letter-sized paper used by most home printers and copiers, take it to a copy shop that can scale it to your desired size.

2. Affix Stencil Design to Stencil Material

Working in a well-ventilated area and following the instructions on the spray adhesive's label, lightly spray the back of the paper printout of your stencil design with adhesive to keep the image from shifting as you cut. Then affix the paper to your transparent film or pennant felt, centering it with an approximate 3-inch border all around.

3. Cut Out Stencil Design

Place the film or felt on a cutting mat with your design facing up. Use the tip of the craft knife to cut out all the black areas of the design and create a stencil that's a negative image of your original piece of art. Work carefully and slowly to avoid injury.

Cutting Out a Stencil Design

Cut out stencil shapes with a craft knife.

4. Test Stencil

To test a stencil before transferring the image to your project fabric, lay the stencil on top of a piece of paper or transparent film, and use your favorite method of stencil transfer (see page 42) to fill entirely all the areas that you cut out. The resulting image shows exactly how your stencil will look on your fabric. You've also created a backup image that can be cut into a new stencil if the original gets lost or damaged.

Stenciling Materials

A stencil can be made from just about any material since you're simply removing a negative space from this material so that you can paint the fabric underneath. I've made stencils, for example, from poster board, wax paper, and even brown paper bags, but my favorite stencil materials are clear Mylar film and pennant felt.

Clear Mylar Film Available at craft stores, transparent Mylar film comes in various weights, is easy to cut, and can be used with any stencil-transfer method. I recommend using the medium- or heavyweight film, which is easier to work with for stenciling than the thin film. Since this film is transparent, you can also trace a pattern directly on it with a permanent marker or use spray adhesive to affix a design printed on paper. While this film holds up well over time, be careful when storing it because it's very flexible; too much bending can damage it.

Pennant Felt Made from acrylic fibers and available from specialty catalogs and online stores, pennant felt gets its name because it's often used for school pennants. I use it for making stencils because it's thin and sturdy, cuts easily with a craft knife, and produces flexible, durable stencils.

Using a Stencil to Create Single, Repeating, and Allover Designs

Once you have your chosen stencil in hand, you will need to decide where you are going to place the stencil design on your cut project pieces or fabric. For some projects, you might want to transfer a single repeat of your stencil. For example, in the top illustration of the Gore Skirt at right, the skirt is shown with a single repeat of the Angie's Fall stencil. Or, you might want to transfer your stencil design more than once, as shown in the center skirt illustration. Another option is to cover your fabric completely with the stencil design to create an allover pattern. If you're working with a relatively small piece of fabric and a large stencil, that single stencil may produce an allover pattern, as the Large Medallion stencil does on the Medallion Boudoir Pillow on page 109. But, if you're working with a large piece of fabric and a small stencil, then you'll have to either transfer your stencil design multiple times or make your own large stencil. To save time, at Alabama Chanin, we create 18" x 24" allover stencils; they are large enough to cover the body of most T-shirts and yet easy to handle and store. We build a 3" border into the edge of all of our stencils to prevent textile paint from "bleeding" beyond the stenciled area and also to strengthen the stencil itself (see the illustration at bottom right). If you want to create your own allover stencil, you can make it any size that feels comfortable to you.

Gore Skirt with One Repeat of Angie's Fall Stencil

Creating a Large Angie's Fall Stencil for Allover Designs

Gore Skirt with Two Repeats of Angie's Fall Stencil

Gore Skirt with Angie's Fall Stencil as Allover Design

Stencil-Transfer Methods

Following are instructions for our basic stencil-transfer methods, plus variations we've used in our recent collections. These techniques create amazing fabrics and allow for endless exploration.

Getting Started (All Methods)

To get started with each technique, you'll need to prepare your work surface and the stencil itself, and also correctly position the stencil on your protected work surface.

1. Prepare Work Surface

Cover your work surface with a sheet, towel, or large scrap of fabric to protect it. This will also keep your garment fabric stable and in place when you're transferring the stencil. Lay your fabric, right side up, on top of the covered work surface.

2. Prepare Stencil

Apply a light coating of spray adhesive on the back of your stencil to keep it from slipping during the transfer process. Then proceed with the directions given for each transfer method.

Stencil Transfer with Permanent and Textile Markers

Transferring stencil patterns to fabric with permanent and textile markers is easy but time-consuming. Permanent markers come in a variety of colors, and the marks they make last through many washings (except for the color red, which bleeds in the wash). An alternative to permanent markers, textile markers are now available in a variety of styles and colors at most hobby shops and art stores. Take care to read all the instructions included with textile markers since some varieties require heat-setting to prevent transferred color from washing out. With all varieties of markers, do a small sample and perform a wash test before using on an actual project.

Supplies

Stencil

Cotton-jersey fabric

Permanent or textile marker

Spray adhesive

1. Trace Stencil

After preparing your work surface and stencil, and correctly positioning your fabric on the covered work surface, use your marker of choice to carefully transfer the stencil onto the project, tracing around the interior outline of each individual cut-out shape. After tracing the entire stencil and letting the image dry, if you want to create a repeating or an allover design, reposition the stencil adjacent to the first stenciled motif and trace the design again. Repeat this process until you've stenciled the design you desire.

2. Dry and Heat-Set If Required

Let your stenciled image(s) dry completely. If you're using textile markers, follow the manufacturer's directions for heat-setting the transferred stencil to prevent the color from washing out.

More Uses for Markers

I like to use permanent and textile markers to hand-write and embroider on our clothing and home items and on our Textile Stories quilts (see page 160). For our Fall/Winter 2008 Revolution Collection, we hand-wrote messages on coats, jackets, T-shirts, and pillows, then embroidered them using backstitches (see page 23). I recently made a house-warming gift for a friend by embroidering one of our hand-sewn throws with the name of her house, the address, and the date she and her family moved in.

Stencil Transfer with Textile Paints

There's a wide variety of textile paints now available that work well for transferring a stencil design to fabric. And there are several ways to apply the textile paint to the stencil design—with a stencil brush, sponge, spray bottle, and airbrush gun. While all these methods work equally well and add their own character to the design, at Alabama Chanin we work primarily with an airbrush gun.

Whatever method you choose for applying your paints, always test the paints on a scrap of fabric before beginning any project and closely follow all instructions for safety and/or heat-setting provided by the paint supplier. Most paints—and all dyes—adhere to a fabric's fibers through a chemical reaction. Some paints require heat to become set, or permanent, while others simply need to be air-dried. Following the manufacturer's instruction is always the best route.

Applying Paints with Stencil Brushes and Sponges

Stencil brushes come in a wide variety of styles and sizes, but almost any brush will do since the only goal is to get the paint on the fabric, which you could even do with a tool as simple as your hand. To get the best results with the brush or sponge you're using, before starting work on your actual project, experiment by adding varying amounts of water to the paint and then applying it to fabric scraps.

Supplies

Stencil

Cotton-jersey fabric

Textile paint

Stencil brush or sponge

Spray adhesive

1. Transfer Stencil Design

After preparing your work surface and stencil, and correctly positioning your fabric on the covered work surface (see page 42), use the brush or sponge of your choice to carefully transfer the stencil to the fabric by dabbing paint in each of the stencil's cut-out shapes. When you've finished painting the entire stencil, remove it and let the paint dry to the touch.

Then, if you want to repeat the stencil design or create an allover pattern, reposition the stencil adjacent to the first stenciled motif, paint the design again, and let it dry. Repeat this process until you've created the design you want.

2. Dry and Heat-Set If Required

Let your stenciled project dry completely. We normally allow 24 hours for our textile paint (which does not require heat-setting) to air-dry before beginning any additional embellishment or sewing. If you're working with paints that require heat-setting to become permanent, always follow the manufacturer's directions in order to prevent the transferred color from washing out. Also note that if you're working with paints that air-dry, we don't recommend washing the stenciled fabric for up to three weeks so that the paint can cure completely (this doesn't apply to heat-set paints).

Applying Paint with Spray Bottles and Airbrush Guns

We sometimes recycle spray bottles from our office to spray textile paint on a stencil, but we're always careful to clean out any residue in the bottle since it can affect how the paint adheres to the fabric. Spray bottles come in a variety of shapes and sizes with many types of nozzles, triggers, and on/off devices; simply choose from what you have readily available. We find that the spray bottles with manually adjustable nozzles work best. Before transferring your stencil to your project fabric, play with various mixtures of paint and water to get a wide range of painting effects to choose from. You'll quickly figure out which combination suits your taste, spray bottle, and project.

For serious crafters, I recommend an airbrush gun for transferring stencils since it is easy to operate, provides good paint coverage, and can be used over and over again with a variety of colors and paint mixtures. We use the most basic and least expensive hobby airbrush we can find with a simple air compressor from our local hardware store. For years, we've worked with a 6-gallon, 150 PSI (pounds per square inch) electric air compressor.

Avoid buying an airbrush designed for large coverage, such as for cars and walls, since you'll end up getting paint everywhere you don't want it. You'll also need to play with the PSI on your compressor to get the right settings. This is the tricky part to airbrushing and can take some time and concentration to sort out; but, once you have your settings adjusted to your liking, your airbrush should be easy to use and run smoothly for many years.

When using an airbrush, it's important to keep all of its parts clean and free of dried paint. It's always a good idea to wash up quickly after finishing with the airbrush and keep your paint stored in air-tight containers no longer than three months. Paint will start to dry and clot immediately and, as it dries, can produce small particles that can clog up your airbrush.

Supplies

Stencil

Cotton-jersey fabric

Textile paint

Spray bottle or airbrush gun

Spray adhesive

1. Transfer Stencil Design

After preparing your work surface and stencil, and correctly positioning your fabric on the covered work surface (see page 42), use your spray bottle or airbrush gun to carefully transfer the stencil onto the fabric by spraying paint inside each of the stencil's cut-out shapes. When you've finished painting the entire stencil, remove the stencil, and let the paint dry to the touch.

After the paint has dried, if you want to repeat the stencil design or create an allover pattern, reposition the stencil adjacent to the first stenciled motif, paint the design again, and let the paint dry. Repeat this process until you have created the design you want.

2. Dry and Heat-Set If Required
Finish by letting your stenciled design dry completely. We normally allow 24 hours for our textile paint (which does not require heat-setting) to air-dry before beginning any additional embellishment or sewing. If you're working with paints that require heat-setting to become permanent, always follow the manufacturer's directions in order to prevent the transferred color from washing out. Also note that if you're working with paints that air-dry, we don't recommend washing the stenciled fabric for up to three weeks so that the paint can cure completely (this doesn't apply to heat-set paints).

Washed-Black Stenciling

This stenciling technique uses watered-down textile paint to lightly stain the fabric when transferring a stencil. We call this washed-black stenciling because we've found that it works best with the color black. This technique gives a subtle patterning to the ground of any project.

Supplies

Stencil

Cotton-jersey fabric

Textile paint

Water

Spray bottle

Spray adhesive

1. Prepare Paint
Mix 3 parts textile paint to 1 part water in a spray bottle.

2. Transfer Stencil Design
After preparing your work surface and stencil and correctly positioning your fabric on the covered work surface (see page 42), position your stencil; then spray the mixture through the stencil onto the fabric (note that you'll get different effects by holding the spray bottle at varying distances from the fabric). After stenciling one area, wait for the paint to dry to the touch, then move the stencil to the next area to be stenciled and repeat the process. Allow the fabric to dry for 24 hours (once it's dry to the touch, you can hang it or leave it flat on your worktable). Then wash and dry the fabric in your washer and dryer.

Wet-Paint Stenciling

Wet-paint stenciling is a technique that we developed to color fabric and add a stencil pattern at the same time. The result is beautiful and has the quality of watercolor painting. We used the wet-painted stencil technique to create the Faded Leaves effect in many of the projects in this book, and you'll find the directions for it in the box, opposite. Note that we've been able to produce positive results with wet-paint stenciling only using darker paints and that we've had the most success with black.

At Alabama Chanin, we generally wet-paint 4½ yards of fabric at a time (the size of two of our Dinner-on-the-Ground Tables on page 130 pushed together side by side). If, however, your work area only allows for painting smaller pieces, simply cut the fabric into pieces large enough to accommodate the size of your project's pattern pieces. Then paint all the pieces in one session since it's hard to duplicate painting results exactly from one session to the next (which is part of what I love about this technique).

Supplies

Stencil

Cotton-jersey fabric

Black textile paint

Container large enough for soaking fabric

Water (enough to cover your fabric in the container you use)

Table salt (4–6 tablespoons per yard of fabric)

Airbrush or spray bottle for paint

Spray bottle for water

Drop cloth

1. Soak Fabric
Combine the water and salt in a container large enough to cover your fabric. Add the fabric and soak for at least 20 minutes; this will open the fabric's fibers to receive the textile paint. Drain and wring the excess water from the fabric.

2. Transfer Stencil Design
After preparing your work surface and stencil and correctly positioning your fabric on the covered work surface (see page 42), position your stencil on the wet fabric and use either an airbrush or spray bottle to spray black textile paint over the stencil. Move the stencil to the next area to be painted while the fabric and paint are still wet, and repeat the process as often as needed to stencil the entire desired area.

3. Spray Fabric with Water

While the fabric and paint are still wet, use a clean spray bottle filled with water to spray the entire length of your painted fabric, which will cause the fabric paint to disperse and bleed. Let the wet fabric sit for 1 hour.

4. Dry and Wash Fabric

Hang the wet fabric to dry for 24 hours outside or indoors over a drop cloth to protect the surface beneath (dripping excess water and paint can cause staining). Wash the fabric in the washing machine with detergent for one wash cycle to remove the excess paint. Dry the fabric in the machine, or hang it to air-dry.

After this wet-painted fabric has dried thoroughly, you can use it as is for a project or embroider or otherwise embellish it, as we did for the Medallion Boudoir Pillow on page 109 and the Basic Tank Dress on page 69. While we like to use natural-color cotton jersey for our projects, you can choose any color base fabric. But keep in mind that a lighter-color base will show your faded-paint effect more clearly (see the example at right).

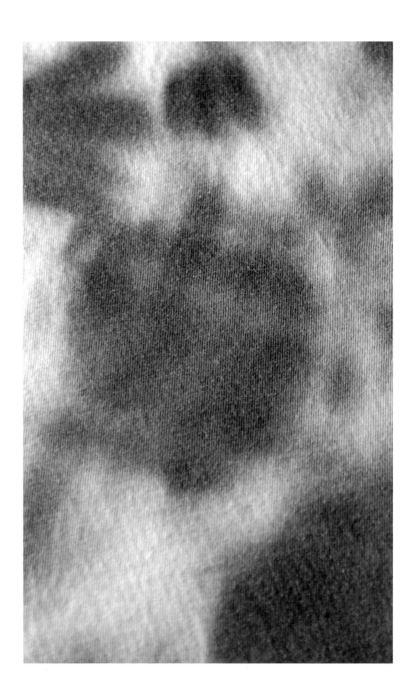

Our Faded Leaves Effect

We used this wet-paint stenciling technique to create the effect we call Faded Leaves for many of the projects in this book. To make Faded Leaves, we start with natural-color cotton-jersey fabric and wet-paint it (see the instructions above) using black textile paint and the Angie's Fall stencil to create an allover pattern.

Appliqué

When I first started crafting as a little girl in the late 1960s, I used fusible adhesive to create all sorts of iron-on appliqués. I vividly recall cutting out apple, butterfly, and flower shapes and ironing them onto bags, blue jeans, T-shirts, and just about anything else I could get my hands on.

I never would have guessed back then that appliqué would become an integral part of my adult career, but it is, in fact, one of the cornerstones of our work at Alabama Chanin. We used it throughout *Alabama Stitch Book*. And here we present three of our newer appliqué techniques: circle-spiral appliqué, relief appliqué, and backstitched reverse appliqué. Whatever your choice of technique, it's a good idea to make a sample to practice the method before working with your project fabric.

As you stitch these appliqués, you'll notice that each shape starts and ends with a fresh knot. It may seem like a lot of work to tie so many knots, but it is well worth the effort as it ensures that your completed garment will retain its stretch.

Circle-Spiral Appliqué

Circle-spiral appliqué (shown in the photo opposite) involves cutting out a random circle, spiral-cutting into the center of the circle, and then sewing the resulting spiral down to a base fabric with a straight stitch (see page 22). We don't measure anything when cutting the circle spiral but simply cut by eye, which adds varied character to the appliqués that we love. We used this appliqué technique for our Fall/Winter 2008/09 Revolution Collection, and it can be applied to any project—dresses, pillows, chairs, drapes, and T-shirts. To add variation to this technique, use scraps from your wet-paint stenciling (see page 48) for your appliqué.

Supplies

Stencil

Cotton-jersey base fabric

Cotton-jersey appliqué fabric

Cotton-jersey backing fabric (if your project calls for it)

Embroidery scissors

Garment scissors

Ruler

Hand-sewing needle

Button craft thread

Pins

1. Cut Out Circle

Using garment scissors, cut out a circle any size you want from your appliqué fabric. For the projects in this book, we used both 3"- to 4"-diameter and 7"- to 8"-diameter circles. Depending on the size circle you choose, cut the number of circles needed to cover the area to be appliquéd. If you're not comfortable cutting circles freehand, use a compass or a jar, plate, or other circular object as a guide.

2. Cut Spiral Appliqué

Place your garment scissors at a 45-degree angle to the edge of one of your cut circles, and cut into the circle by $\frac{1}{2}$". Working freestyle, continue cutting in a spiral, first cutting about $\frac{1}{2}$" from the outside edge and then cutting in towards the center, always keeping about a $\frac{1}{2}$" space between the cutting lines. Stop cutting when you have about a 1"-diameter circle left in the center of your spiral. Repeat the process with each of your remaining cut circles.

3. Pin Appliqué to Project

Randomly place and pin your cut spiral appliqués on the base fabric, slightly overlapping the edges by about $\frac{1}{8}$".

4. Stitch Appliqué Spiral to Base Fabric

Use a straight stitch to sew the appliqué spiral to the base fabric: Begin stitching along the edge of the 1"-diameter circle in the center of the appliqué, and then stitch outwards along the edge of the spiral cut. When you reach about $\frac{1}{8}$" from the end of the spiral's outside point, turn and stitch your way back to your starting point at the center 1"-diameter circle, where you'll knot off your thread.

Relief Appliqué

Relief appliqué is a very simple technique that entails appliquéing a piece of fabric onto a slightly smaller stenciled base shape, which creates a beautiful, textured surface. Note that this technique requires preparing two sets of stencils: one for the base fabric and a second one for the appliqué itself that's a 15% enlargement of the appliqué elements (produced on a photocopier) of the first stencil.

Supplies

Stencil for base

Stencil for appliqué: base stencil enlarged by 15%

Cotton-jersey base fabric

Cotton-jersey appliqué fabric

Cotton-jersey backing fabric (if your project calls for it)

Sharpie marker or textile spray paint

Embroidery scissors

Hand-sewing needle

Button craft thread

Pins

1. Stencil Pattern on Base Fabric

On the right side of your base fabric, stencil your base pattern where you want to place the appliqué pieces (see page 42).

2. Stencil Pattern on Appliqué Fabric

Working with your second, enlarged stencil, flip the stencil to the wrong side (that is, opposite from the base stencil), and position it on the wrong side (back) of the appliqué fabric. Transfer the stencil on the appliqué fabric's wrong side as many times as you stenciled the base stencil on the base fabric. Then cut out each of the medium and large appliqué shapes in your design; and, as you work, pin the center of each cut appliqué, right side up, to its matching shape on the right side of the base fabric.

3. Attach Backing-Fabric Layer to Top-Fabric Layer

If your project calls for using a layer of backing fabric, which will be cut to the full size of your pattern pieces, place the cut backing fabric, right side up, behind the top layer of fabric to be appliquéd, making sure that the grain lines (see page 11) on both fabrics run in the same direction. Pin the two pieces together securely.

4. Whipstitch Medium and Large Appliqué Shapes to Stenciled Design

Since the appliqué shapes are 15% larger than the stenciled shapes on the base fabric, you'll have to ease in each appliqué's excess fabric by pinning its edge to align with the edge of each smaller corresponding stenciled shape. Using a parallel whipstitch (see page 25), sew around each appliqué's pinned, cut edge to secure the appliqué to the base fabric.

5. Iron Fabric to Create Relief

Use a steam iron to gently iron your work, pushing lightly down on the fabric to flatten the appliqué pieces, which will cause them to fold in upon themselves and create the relief effect.

6. Backstitch Stenciled Design's Small Shapes

Because the small areas of a stenciled design on the base fabric are difficult to cover with relief appliqué, we simply highlight those areas by backstitching (see page 23) around them (or using another embroidery stitch to stitch around them) without any additional appliqué (see the detail photo at left).

Backstitched Reverse Appliqué

Reverse appliqué consists of two layers of fabric—a stenciled top layer and a backing layer—that are stitched together along the edges of the stenciled designs. Then part of the top layer of fabric is cut away within the stitched areas to reveal the backing fabric underneath.

Backstitched reverse appliqué is a variation of reverse appliqué that uses the backstitch (see page 23) rather than the traditional straight stitch to attach the two layers of fabric. This technique creates a stunning effect since each shape of your stenciled design is completely outlined. But be aware that this technique uses three times as much thread as basic reverse appliqué and takes about twice as long to complete.

While embroidery floss is not a good choice for basic reverse appliqué since it's not as strong as the button craft thread we prefer, it does work well for backstitched reverse appliqué because the extra stitches that make up the backstitch provide additional strength.

Supplies

Stencil

Cotton-jersey base fabric

Cotton-jersey backing fabric in different color

Textile paint

Embroidery scissors

Hand-sewing needle

Button craft thread or embroidery floss

Pins

1. Transfer Design to Top Fabric

Using stencil-transfer method of your choice (see page 42), transfer your stencil design onto the right side of your top fabric layer.

2. Attach Backing Fabric to Top Fabric

Place the cut backing fabric, right side up, behind the area of the top layer of fabric to be appliquéd, making sure that the grain lines on both fabrics run in the same direction (see page 11). Pin the two fabrics together securely.

3. Stitch Around Stencil Shapes

Prepare your needle using a single strand of thread or two strands of embroidery floss doubled (so that after you make your knot, you are working with two strands of thread or four strands of floss), "love" your thread (see page 12), and knot off (see page 21). Choose one of the shapes in your stenciled design as a starting point, and insert your needle according to the project directions, from either the right side of the top layer (in which case your knot will show on the project's right side) or from the wrong side of the backing layer (in which case the knot will be hidden on the project's wrong side), and pull the thread or floss through the other layer. Then stitch around the shape using a backstitch (see page 23) until you arrive back at your starting point, and knot off your thread or floss using a double knot on the side of the fabric on which you originally inserted your needle.

Move to a neighboring shape and stitch around it as before, tying off your thread or floss with a double knot. Continue to move from one shape to the next, stitching around each one and always tying off with a double knot.

4. Cut Away Inside Top Layer's Stitched Shapes

Insert the tip of your embroidery scissors in the center of one of your stitched shapes, being careful to puncture only the top layer of fabric. Then carefully trim away the inside of the shape, leaving behind only about $\frac{1}{8}$" of fabric alongside your stitched outline. The remaining $\frac{1}{8}$" is wide enough to prevent the fabric and the stitching from unraveling or pulling through and yet narrow enough to display the reverse appliqué pattern nicely (along with a sliver of the original stenciled image's paint color). Make sure not to cut any closer than $\frac{1}{8}$" to your seam, which would cause the fabric to eventually tear away from the stitching and leave a hole in your beautiful work.

After you trim the top layer of fabric on every shape, you have two options for finishing the backing fabric: Either leave the fabric as is, or turn the project wrong side out and trim the backing fabric to leave a narrow border around the entire piece. None of the projects in this book require trimming the backing fabric.

Inked & Quilted

Inked & Quilted is a method we developed for our Spring/Summer 2006 Circus Collection to replace our standard reverse appliqué. It looks very similar to reverse appliqué, but, because it requires no cutting of appliqués or backing fabric, it works up much more quickly. Note that rather than stitching right along the edge of the inked shape, this method calls for stitching ⅛" inside that edge.

Supplies

Stencil

Cotton-jersey fabric

Cotton-jersey backing fabric (if your project calls for it)

Textile paint

Fine-point black permanent marker

Embroidery scissors

Hand-sewing needle

Button craft thread

Pins

1. Transfer Design to Top

Using textile paint, transfer the stencil design (see page 44) to the right side of the cut top layer of your project.

2. Attach Backing Fabric to Top Fabric

If your project calls for using a layer of backing fabric, which you'll cut to the full size of your pattern pieces, place the cut backing fabric, right side up, behind the area of the top layer of fabric to be appliquéd, making sure that the grain lines (see page 11) on both fabrics run in the same direction. Pin the two fabrics together securely.

3. Trace Around Shapes with Marker

Using a fine-point permanent marker, carefully trace around the outside edge of every stenciled shape.

4. Stitch Inside Stencil Shapes

Thread your needle with a double strand of thread, "love" your thread (see page 12), and knot off with a double knot (see page 21). Choose one of the shapes in your stenciled design as a starting point, and insert your needle according to the project directions, from either the right side of the top layer (in which case your knot will show on the project's right side) or from the wrong side of the backing layer (in which case the knot will be hidden on the project's wrong side), and pull the thread through both layers. Then, using a straight stitch (see page 22), stitch ⅛" from the edge of the appliqué shape until you arrive back at your starting point. Knot off your thread using a double knot on the side of the fabric on which you originally inserted your needle.

Move to a neighboring shape and stitch around it as before, tying off your thread with a double knot. Continue moving from one shape to the next, stitching inside each one and always tying off with a double knot.

String Quilting

String quilting is one of my all-time favorite techniques because it so elegantly combines hand-sewing with the best principle of sustainable design—recycling what would ordinarily be thrown away.

My former neighbor, Mrs. Killen, once told me that they did not have a garbage can at her house when she was growing up. "We used every scrap we could," she said, "and what we could not use went for either compost or feeding the livestock." This is a beautiful concept, taking the scraps from everyday life and giving them a new use. There's an old saying that I've heard quilters in my community use: "This one was scraped together."

This technique was originally worked with pieces of paper used as the foundation on which small—and even tiny—fabric scraps were "stringed," or sewn, together into the shape of a desired quilt block. After the quilt block was sewn, the paper was removed from the back and discarded, and the individual quilt blocks were eventually sewn together to form the quilt. In our version of string quilting, we use a piece of fabric as the foundation pattern and appliqué scraps to it, creating a firm base that becomes a part of the final project.

Supplies

Project pattern

Cotton-jersey fabric

Four to five cotton-jersey scraps 1"–2" longer than your project pattern piece

Garment scissors

Embroidery scissors

18" transparent plastic ruler

Rotary cutter and cutting mat

Tailor's chalk or disappearing-ink fabric pen

Hand-sewing needle

Button craft thread

Pins

1. Cut Strips for "String"

Using the transparent ruler, rotary cutter, and cutting mat, begin cutting strips from your cotton-jersey scraps, as follows (if you're using different colored fabric or scraps, cut strips from all the different colors): Align the ruler with the fabric's grain line (see page 11), and hold it tightly in place to use as a guide for the rotary cutter. Cutting lengthwise with the grain line of the jersey, cut the strips in varying widths, making sure they're each at least 1" or 2" longer than your project pattern piece and that none is narrower than $\frac{5}{8}$" (if they're narrower, they'll be difficult to stitch). As few as three strips can make a beautiful project piece, or you may want to string-quilt a multitude of strips.

2. Cut Out Foundation Pattern

Place the cotton-jersey fabric you want to use for the project's foundation pattern right side up. Lay the pattern pieces on the fabric, matching the pattern's and fabric's grain lines, and trace around each pattern piece with tailor's chalk. Remove the pattern, and cut out your pattern pieces (see page 36), making sure to cut in a smooth line just inside of the chalked line so that you remove it entirely.

3. String-Quilt Pattern Pieces

Working with one foundation pattern piece at a time, lay the pattern piece right side up and then lay the first cut strip, right side up, on the left edge of the pattern piece, making sure the fabric strip covers the pattern piece's left edge from top to bottom (see illustration at left, below).

Lay the second strip, wrong side up, on top of first strip, aligning the right edges of the two strips (see illustration at center, below).

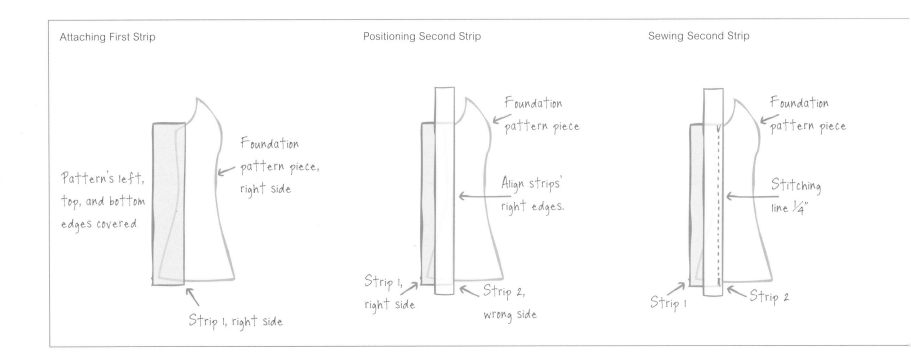

Attaching First Strip

Foundation pattern piece, right side

Pattern's left, top, and bottom edges covered

Strip 1, right side

Positioning Second Strip

Foundation pattern piece

Align strips' right edges.

Strip 1, right side

Strip 2, wrong side

Sewing Second Strip

Foundation pattern piece

Stitching line ¼"

Strip 1

Strip 2

Using a straight stitch (see page 22), join these two strips and the foundation piece, sewing $\frac{1}{4}$" from their aligned, raw, right edges through both layers of fabric and the foundation (see illustration at right, opposite page).

Fold back the second strip to the right side to reveal a clean-finished seam. Repeat the process of joining a new strip, attaching it, again with right sides together, to the right edge of the second strip. Continue adding new strips this way until you've covered the full width of the foundation pattern piece (see below).

As you work, make sure that your knots are tight, that your stitches are a consistent length, and that you start and end each seam $\frac{1}{8}$" from the top and bottom edges of the foundation pattern piece. Carefully trim away any excess fabric overhanging the foundation pattern piece, then repeat the string-quilting process for the remaining foundation pattern pieces to be string-quilted.

Note that if you want to stencil your string-quilted fabric, as we did in the String-Quilted & Stenciled Tank Top on page 127, now is the time to choose your stencil pattern and transfer it with textile paint to your string-quilted pattern pieces.

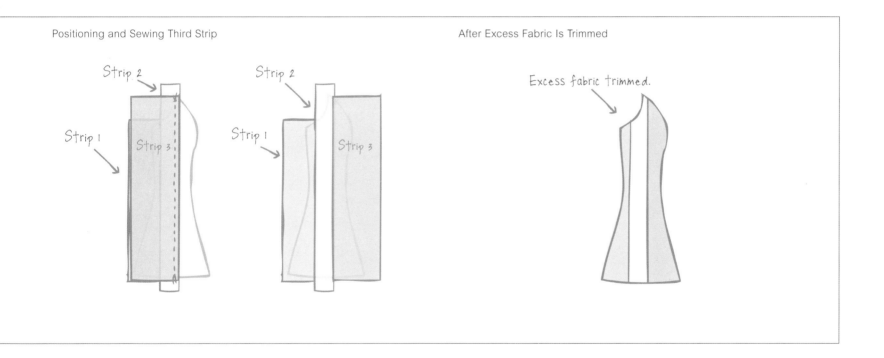

Positioning and Sewing Third Strip

Strip 2
Strip 1
Strip 3

Strip 2
Strip 1
Strip 3

After Excess Fabric Is Trimmed

Excess fabric trimmed.

Alabama Chanin Eyelets

At Alabama Chanin, we use the term *eyelet* for stitches worked around a circular point, although it more typically denotes a small decorative or utilitarian hole. For our Spring/Summer 2009 Ceremony Collection, we combined buttonhole eyelets, whipped eyelets, and beaded eyelets. The photograph at right shows these eyelet variations, and basic instructions for stitching them follow.

Supplies

Fabric for top layer

Fabric for backing layer

Disappearing-ink fabric pen

Embroidery scissors

Hand-sewing needle

Button craft thread or embroidery floss

Beads (for working beaded eyelets only)

Pins

1. Draw Design on Top Fabric

Using a disappearing-ink pen, draw circles or dots in the desired sizes where you want to create eyelets.

Mark Eyelet Positions and Size

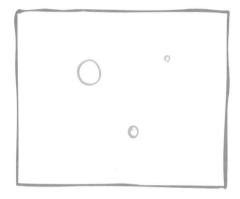

2. Attach Backing Fabric to Top Fabric

Place the cut backing fabric, right side up, behind the area of the top layer of fabric where the eyelets will be sewn making sure that both fabrics' grain lines run in the same direction (see page 11). Pin the two pieces together securely.

Attach Backing and Top Fabrics

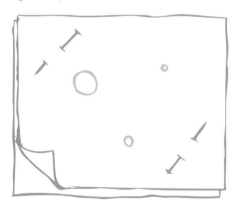

3. Stitch Eyelets Around Drawn Shapes

Prepare your needle using a single strand of thread or two strands of embroidery floss doubled (so that after you make your knot, you are working with two strands of thread or four strands of floss), "love" your thread (see page 12), and knot off (see page 21). Choose one of your drawn shapes as a starting point, and insert your needle according to the project directions, from either the right side of the top layer (in which case your knot will show on the project's right side) or from the wrong side of the backing layer (in which case the knot will show on the project's wrong side), pulling the thread through the other layer. Then stitch around the shape using a parallel whipstitch (see page 25), or adding a bead to your stitch (see page 65), depending on the kind of eyelet you want to make. Continue stitching until you arrive back at your starting point, and knot off your thread with a double knot on the same side of the fabric where you originally inserted your needle.

Move to a neighboring shape and stitch around it as before, tying off your thread with a double knot. Repeat the process, moving from one shape to the next, always tying off with a double knot, until you've sewn all the drawn eyelets.

Embroider Each Eyelet Separately

Knot off thread with a double knot after sewing each eyelet.

Beading

Beads come in a variety of materials, shapes, and sizes. I favor glass beads because they're readily available, sold in an array of colors, and have a beautiful luster. At Alabama Chanin, we use mainly bugle beads (elongated cylindrical beads), chop beads (a small version of bugle beads), and seed beads (very small, rounded beads).

You can bead either a single layer or several layers of fabric. Since you'll treat the multiple layers as a unit, that is, as a single layer, the beading process is the same either way.

Cluster Beading

Cluster beading is our term for attaching beads so that they appear to have been randomly dropped in clusters onto a project, as shown in the photographs on pages 156 and 166.

Supplies Needed

Glass bugle beads and seed beads

Button craft thread

Millinery needle with large eye

1. Prepare Needle and Thread

Thread your beading needle, "love" your thread (see page 12), and knot off (see page 21).

2. Sew Beaded Stitches

Insert your needle into the right side of your fabric (or the wrong side if you want to hide the knots). Take one stitch, bringing your needle up to the right side; insert it through one to three beads, depending on how many will fit—or you decide to use—on your stitch, and take another stitch, bringing your needle up on the right side again. Continue inserting your needle through one or more beads, stitching, and pulling your thread through to the right side of the fabric.

You can place beads on every stitch, every other stitch, or every fifth (for example) stitch; or you can place beads randomly throughout your project. You can combine cluster beading with French knots, eyelets, or beaded eyelets, or other beaded stitches as well.

Beaded Embroidery Stitches

There are as many variations of beaded stitches as there are stitches and varieties of beads. When using this technique, you're only limited by your imagination and the size of the bead. Here are three of our favorite beaded stitches.

Beaded Rosebud The beaded rosebud is an all-time favorite among our stitches. We used it for the first time in our Fall/Winter 2008/09 Revolution Collection. To work this stitch, add four seed beads to every loop of the rosebud stitch (see page 25).

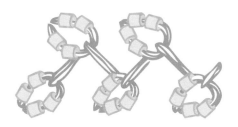

Beaded Whipstitch For a beaded whipstitch, add one bugle bead or three seed beads to every parallel whipstitch (see page 25). The stitches can be sewn tightly together or loosely spaced.

Beaded Eyelets For a beaded eyelet, use a whipstitch to sew bugle beads around a center point, which will give the illusion of a sewn eyelet.

Note: For the projects in this book that call for the Small Medallion stencil, you can use the pull-out stencil inserted between pages 144 and 145, or you can photocopy the artwork shown here at 100 percent. For projects that call for the Large Medallion stencil, you'll need to photocopy and enlarge this artwork by 335 percent. Or you can download this artwork full-size from www.alabamachanin.com.

Chapter 4 | Projects & Recipes

Now that you've reviewed the materials, stitches, and techniques that are at the core of our work, you are ready to create your own couture projects to wear and to decorate your home. Here you will find simple projects that work up quickly and more elaborate ones that require more time. In between the projects are tips, treats, and recipes to enrich the experience. I hope you will enjoy the process of making these projects as much as the final products themselves and that what you see here will inspire you to create lasting beauty for yourself, your home, and your community.

Basic Tank Dress

While I love our highly embroidered dresses, I'm equally enamored with our versatile and flattering basic designs. For this one, I worked the seams—which really come to the forefront when there's no elaborate stitch work to compete with—in matching button craft thread and then felled the seam allowances open using a whipstitch and embroidery floss. Other stitches that work well for open-felling are straight, herringbone, and rosebud. This is the perfect dress for summer outings, beach trips, and dinners out. I even wear it while gardening. I have it in several colors and wear it constantly.

Our Design Choices

Dress fabric — **Faded Leaves**

Thread — **Grey**

Stretch stitch — **Herringbone**

Seams — **Open-felled on right side**

Felling stitch — **Parallel whipstitch**

Knots — **Inside garment**

Supplies

Tank Dress pattern (see pattern sheet at back of book)

3 yards of 60"-wide natural cotton-jersey fabric

Angie's Fall stencil (see page 31)

Supplies for Faded Leaves stenciling (see page 48)

Paper scissors

Garment scissors

Rotary cutter and cutting mat

18" transparent plastic ruler

Tailor's chalk or disappearing-ink fabric pen

Hand-sewing needle

Button craft thread

All-purpose sewing thread

Pins

1. Color Fabric with Faded Leaves

Following the instructions on page 48, wet-paint stencil your cotton jersey, and let the fabric dry thoroughly.

2. Prepare and Cut Pattern

Photocopy or trace the Tank Dress pattern on the pattern sheet, and use your paper scissors to cut the traced or photocopied pattern in your desired size (see page 37), cutting as close as possible to the black cutting lines. Note that the Center Front and Center Back pattern pieces are half-patterns, which are meant to be cut on folded fabric with the pattern edge marked "Place on fold" positioned accordingly. Note, too, that all the pattern pieces have a ¼" seam allowance built into the edges, except for the neckline, armhole, and hem edges, which, for this dress, are left raw, with the neckline and armhole then bound.

The Tank Dress has a total of six pattern pieces: 1 Center Front, 2 Side Fronts, 1 Center Back, and 2 Side Backs.

For cutting the Center Front and Center Back pattern pieces, lay your fabric out single layer and right side up. Make sure when positioning the pattern pieces on your fabric that the fabric's and pattern's grain lines (see page 11) run in the same direction. Using tailor's chalk, trace around the pattern's edges. Then remove the pattern and cut it out, cutting in a smooth line just inside the chalked line so that you remove it entirely.

When cutting the two Side Fronts and two Side Backs, you can layer two pieces of cotton jersey right side up, and cut out the two needed pieces at once. Make sure when positioning the two layers that the fabric grain on each layer runs in the same direction. Likewise be sure to position the pattern piece on the two layers so that the fabrics' and pattern's grain lines run in the same direction. When finished, you will have a total of six cut-fabric pattern pieces.

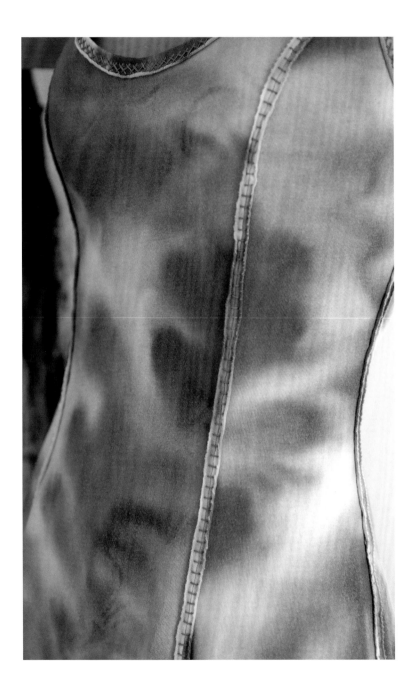

3. Baste Neck and Armholes

Using a single strand of all-purpose thread, baste (see page 22) all the neckline and armhole edges on the cut pattern pieces, as indicated on the pattern pieces, to prevent these edges from stretching while you're working on your Tank Dress.

4. Assemble Front and Back Pieces

With wrong sides together and the cut edges aligned, pin one Side Front piece to each side of the Center Front piece. Following the instructions for open-felling seams on the right side on page 29 and using a straight stitch (see page 22) for the seam itself, begin sewing the pinned pieces together ¼" from the raw edges, starting at the top edge of the Tank Dress. Wrap-stitch (see page 29) the beginning and end of every seam to secure it. As you sew, make sure to check your thread tension, so the fabric lies flat before you tie off the thread at the end of your seam. For open-felling the seam's allowances on this dress, we used a parallel whipstitch (see page 25), though you could also use another decorative stitch (see right).

Repeat the process above to join the three pieces of the Tank Dress's back, stitching one Side Back panel to each side of the Center Back panel.

5. Assemble Tank Dress

With wrong sides together and the cut edges aligned, pin the shoulder seams of the Tank Dress's completed front and back panels. Using a straight stitch, sew the shoulders together with a ¼" seam, wrap-stitching the seam and checking your sewing tension, as you did when sewing the seams in Step 4. With wrong sides together, pin and join the dress's sides as you did for the shoulder seams. When finished, carefully iron each seam's allowances open.

6. Bind Neckline and Armholes

Follow the directions in Step 9 of the Inked & Quilted Camisole Dress on page 121 to prepare and attach the binding in place on the dress's neckline and armholes.

Decorative Stitches for Open-Felled Seams
Shown here are open-felled seams worked with rosebud (left) and herringbone (right) stitches. See pages 24 and 25 for instructions for working them.

String-Quilted Pillow

During the Depression, resources were scarce, and most people could not afford to create quilts from new fabrics. Instead, fabric scraps became valuable tools for constructing quilts necessary to keep families warm at night. When scraps were used, they were often sewn together on top of a base paper pattern made from old newspapers, catalogs, or magazine pages. My grandmother still refers to this technique as "stringing." This title may have come from the concept, while she was growing up, that everyone used to just "string along" in their daily lives by piecing together meals from the woods, garden, and barnyard; clothes and quilts from sacks and leftovers; and houses from materials available right on their land.

Our Design Choices

Pillow fabric — **Faded Leaves**

String-quilting fabric — **Faded Leaves**

Piping fabric — **Burgundy**

Stencil — **Angie's Fall**

Paint — **White**

Thread — **Grey**

Knots — **Inside pillow**

Finished Size: 20" square

Supplies

One 20" square and one 20" x 16" piece of pattern paper or butcher paper (see page 14)

1¼ yards of 60"-wide, natural cotton-jersey fabric

⅛ yard of 60"-wide, cotton-jersey fabric in contrasting color, for piping

Angie's Fall stencil (see page 31)

Supplies for Faded Leaves stenciling (see page 48)

Textile paint

Tools for your choice of stencil-transfer method (see page 42)

One pair each of garment, embroidery, and paper scissors

Rotary cutter and cutting mat

18" transparent plastic ruler

Tailor's chalk or disappearing-ink fabric pen

Hand-sewing needle

Button craft thread

Pins

20" pillow form or pillow filling of choice

1. Label Patterns

Using a pencil and ruler, draw a line parallel to any side on the 20" square of lightweight pattern paper or butcher paper, and label the line "Grain Line" and the square itself "String Pillow Front."

On the 20" x 16" piece of pattern paper, draw a line parallel to the long sides, and label it "Grain Line" and the rectangle itself "String Pillow Back."

Labeling Patterns

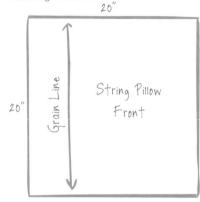
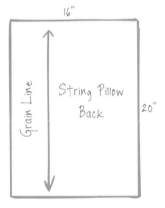

2. Color Fabric with Faded Leaves

Following the directions on page 48, wet-paint stencil your cotton-jersey fabric using the Angie's Fall stencil and black paint to create the Faded Leaves effect on it.

3. Cut Out Pillow Front Base and Back

Cut your dried Faded Leaves fabric in half widthwise, and place the two layers of fabric right side up. Align the two layers, making sure that the grain lines (see page 11) on both pieces run in the same direction. Place the String Pillow Back pattern on top of the two aligned layers, again matching the direction of the pattern's marked grain line with the fabrics' grain lines. Using tailor's chalk, trace around the pattern's edges. Then remove the pattern and cut out two pieces at once, using your rotary cutter and making sure to cut in a smooth line just inside the chalked line so that you remove it entirely. You now have two pillow-back pieces.

Reposition your pattern piece on the remainder of the two fabric layers, and repeat the cutting process above so that you have a total of four pillow-back pieces.

Next lay out a single layer of fabric, right side up, for the pillow front. Position the String Pillow Front pattern on top, making sure that the pattern's and fabric's grain lines run in the same directions. Then trace and cut out the pattern, as explained above.

When finished, you'll have four fabric String Pillow Back pieces and one fabric String Pillow Front.

4. Cut "String" and String Quilt Pillow Front

Following the instructions on page 59, cut your string from the remaining cotton jersey, and string quilt the pillow front.

5. Stencil Design on Pillow Front

Lay the string-quilted Pillow Front right side up, and place the Angie's Fall stencil on top of it. Then, using textile paint and the textile-paint transfer method of your choice, carefully transfer the stencil design onto the string-quilted fabric and let the paint dry to the touch. Next move the stencil to an adjacent area, repeat the process, and continue moving the stencil and painting the fabric until you've stenciled your design over the entire area. Allow the stenciled images to dry thoroughly.

6. Fold and Stitch Edges of Pillow Backs

The back of the pillow is formed by two double-layer pieces that overlap at center back, making it easy to remove the pillow and clean the case. To construct the pillow back, begin by laying the first set of two pillow-back pieces each wrong side up and aligned on top of one another so that the fabrics' grain lines run in the same direction. On one long edge, fold under the two fabric layers together 1" to the wrong side, pin the fold in place, and press the fold with a hot iron to make a crisp edge. Using a straight stitch, stitch ¾" from the folded edge along its length, making sure to wrap-stitch (see page 29) the beginning and end of your seam and also to check your tension as you sew.

Repeat the process above for the second set of pillow-back pieces.

7. Prepare and Pin Piping to Pillow Front

Using the rotary cutter, cutting mat, and large plastic ruler, cut 1¼"-wide fabric strips from your cotton-jersey scraps across the grain to use as the piping around the outside seam of your pillow. You'll need about 82" total of cut strips for the piping.

To make the piping, press the cut strips in half lengthwise, with wrong sides together, using your iron and being careful not to stretch the fabric while pressing it. Starting at the mid-point of one edge of the pillow, pin the folded piping along the edge of the pillow front, aligning the piping's raw edges with the pillow front's raw edge and overlapping the piping's raw ends if you need to add a new piping strip. After pinning piping around the pillow's four edges, overlap the piping's beginning and ending raw ends in a double "U" formation (see the illustration at top right), which helps keep the piping from curling after washing.

Creating Double "U" Formation

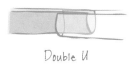

Double U

8. Pin and Stitch Front to Backs

Lay the Pillow Front with the pinned piping right side up. Place the two back pieces on top of the front, wrong side up with the raw edges of the two layers aligned. The back pieces' folded edges will overlap at the center.

Pin the pillow front and back together by removing each pin, securing the piping, and reinserting the pin in place to include the pillow back. Work pin by pin, starting at the four corners and then continuing along each edge between the corners.

Positioning Front and Back Covers for Sewing

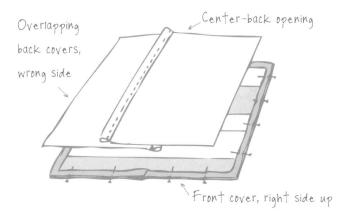

Overlapping back covers, wrong side

Center-back opening

Front cover, right side up

After pinning the front and back together, using a straight stitch (see page 22), insert your needle into the pillow back, and begin stitching the front and back together at the upper right-hand corner, $\frac{1}{4}$" from the raw edge. Be sure to wrap-stitch and knot off at this and the other three corners. Repeat this process until you've sewn around all four edges of the case. Now you have two knots in every corner: one for the beginning of your line of stitching and the other for the end.

Turn your pillowcase right side out and insert the pillow form.

Back Cover, Wrong Side

Opening at center back

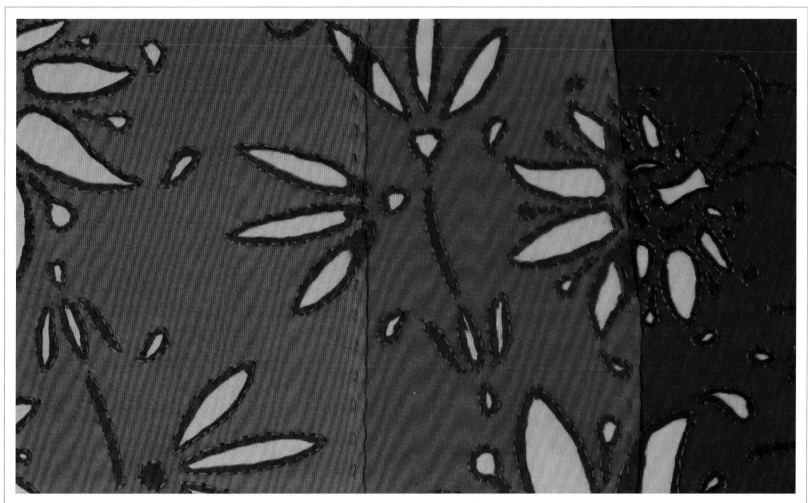

String Quilting with Backstiched Reverse Appliqué

To add an additional layer of detail to our string quilting, we sometimes backstitch reverse appliqué the stencil pattern after painting it on the fabric. To do this, simply use wider strips of fabric for your string quilting—the pieces pictured here measure approximately 6" to 8" in width—transfer your stencil pattern using the stencil-transfer method of choice, then backstitch reverse appliqué (see page 54), making sure not to cut through the areas of your seamed string quilting. After completing your backstitch reverse appliqué, construct your project as usual.

Tank Dress with Relief Appliqué

I have adored dresses ever since I was a little girl. As an adult, I love pulling on this single garment in the morning and knowing that I'm nearly ready for the day. I started adding "necklace" details around my dresses many years ago. For this one, a simple stencil design in a contrasting color draws attention—like a piece of jewelry—to the neckline. If desired, you can continue to embellish further even after you have begun to wear the dress.

Our Design Choices

Dress fabric — **Midnight grey**

Appliqué fabric — **Pewter**

Binding fabric — **Midnight grey**

Stencil — **Angie's Fall**

Paint color — **Brown**

Thread — **Grey for construction**
Brown for appliqué &
neckline binding

Embroidery floss for backstitch — **Brown**

Stretch stitch — **Rosebud**

Seams — **Felled on wrong side**

Knots — **Inside garment**

Supplies

Tank Dress pattern (see pattern sheet at back of book)

6 yards of 60"-wide cotton-jersey fabric

About ¼ yard of cotton-jersey scraps, for appliqué

Angie's Fall stencil (see page 31)

Textile paint

Tool of your choice for stencil-transfer method (see page 42)

Paper scissors

Garment scissors

Rotary cutter and cutting mat

18" transparent plastic ruler

Tailor's chalk or disappearing-ink fabric pen

Hand-sewing needle

Button craft thread

All-purpose sewing thread

Pins

1. Prepare and Cut Pattern

Photocopy or trace the Tank Dress pattern, and use your paper scissors to cut the traced or photocopied pattern in your desired size (see page 37), staying as close as possible to the black cutting lines. Note that the Center Front and Center Back pattern pieces are half-patterns, which are meant to be cut on folded fabric with the pattern edge marked "Place on fold" positioned accordingly. Note, too, that all the pattern pieces have a ¼" seam allowance built into the edges, except for the neckline, armhole, and hem edges, which, for this top, are left raw, with the neckline and armholes then bound.

The Tank Dress has a total of six pattern pieces: 1 Center Front, 2 Side Fronts, 1 Center Back, and 2 Side Backs.

You'll cut two fabric pieces for each pattern piece—a top layer and a backing layer—and you can cut these two pieces at the same time by layering two pieces of the cotton jersey right side up. Make sure when positioning the two layers that the grain line (see page 11) on each layer runs in the same direction. Likewise be sure to position the pattern piece on the two layers so that the fabrics' and pattern's grain lines run in the same direction.

Using tailor's chalk, trace around the pattern's edges. Then remove the pattern, and cut out the two pieces at once, using your fabric scissors, and making sure to cut in a smooth line just inside the chalked line so that you remove it entirely.

When finished, you will have a total of 12 cut-fabric pattern pieces.

2. Baste Neck and Armholes

Using a single strand of all-purpose thread, baste (see page 22) all the neckline and armhole edges on the cut pattern pieces, as indicated on the pattern pieces, to prevent these edges from stretching while you're working on your dress.

3. Stencil Design on Pattern Pieces

Place the top layer of the Tank Dress's three front-pattern pieces right side up, positioning each piece adjacent to its neighboring piece, so the stencil pattern will continue unbroken as you stencil the repeats, continuing from one piece of fabric to another. Place the Angie's Fall stencil on one of the two Side Front pieces to start stenciling. Using textile paint and the stencil-transfer method of your choice (see page 42), carefully transfer the edge of the stencil design along the neck edge of the dress (see the photo on page 78), and let the paint dry to the touch. Then reposition the stencil on the center panel, so that the largest flower is centered on the panel, transfer the pattern, and again let the paint dry to the touch. Finally, reposition the edge of the stencil along the neckline on the other side panel, transfer the pattern, and let the paint dry.

Repeat the process on the Tank Dress's three back-pattern pieces, positioning the stencil designs in a pleasing arc below the back neckline, and allow all the stenciled designs to dry thoroughly.

4. Pin Pattern's Top and Backing Layers

Align each top-layer pattern piece on each corresponding backing-layer piece, with both fabrics facing right side up, and pat the layers into place (see page 36) so that their edges are aligned. Securely pin together the edges of both layers on each piece.

5. Stencil Design on Appliqué Fabric

The stencil for your relief-appliqué fabric needs to be a 15-percent enlargement of the Angie's Fall stencil used in Step 3. To create this enlarged stencil and cut out your stenciled appliqué pieces, follow the directions in Step 4 of the Relief Appliqué Chair Pillow on page 154.

6. Relief-Appliqué Medium & Large Shapes

Using your stenciled appliqués from Step 5, follow the instructions for relief appliqué on page 53 to appliqué each medium and large shape of the stenciled design on the dress's front and back.

7. Backstitch Small Shapes in Stenciled Design

Backstitch (see page 23) around each small shape in the stenciled Angie's Fall design on the dress's front and back, but leave these small shapes uncut.

8. Assemble Front and Back Pieces

With the fabric right sides together and the cut edges aligned, pin one Side Front piece to each side of the Center Front piece. Following the instructions for sewing felled seams on the wrong side on page 28 and using a straight stitch (see page 22), begin sewing the pinned pieces together ¼" from the raw edges, starting at the top edge of the Tank Dress. Wrap-stitch (see page 29) the beginning and end of every seam to secure it. As you sew, make sure to check your thread tension, so the fabric lies flat before you tie off the thread at the end of your seam.

Repeat the process above to join the Tank Dress's three back pieces, sewing one Side Back panel to each side of the Center Back panel.

9. Assemble Tank Dress

With right sides together, pin the shoulder seams of the Tank Dress's completed front and back panels. Following the instructions for sewing felled seams on the wrong side on page 28 and using a straight stitch, sew the pinned pieces together ¼" from the raw edges, starting at the top edge of the Tank Dress. As in Step 8, wrap-stitch the beginning and end of the seams to secure them, and check your thread tension as you sew.

With right sides together and the cut edges aligned, pin and join the dress's side edges as you did the shoulder seams.

10. Bind Neckline and Armholes

Follow the directions in Step 9 of the Inked & Quilted Camisole Dress on page 121 to bind the tunic's neckline and armholes.

Eyelet-Embroidered Placemats & Napkins

Placemats, in every material from linen to vinyl, are a standard fixture on the Southern dining table. My grandmother had a set of strangely appealing green vinyl mats that she used on her kitchen table when I was a little girl, which doubtless engendered my fondness for placemats today. The placemats and napkins shown here are very simple and can be made for everyday use in their most basic form, or they can be heavily embroidered for special occasions. The instructions below are for six placemats and matching napkins, but you can increase or reduce the number as desired.

Our Design Choices

Base fabric — **Cream**

Backing fabric — **Cream**

Stripe fabric — **Grey**

Thread — **Cream**

Embroidery floss — **Cream**

Knots — **On wrong side**

Supplies

Pattern paper (see page 14): one 14" x 20" piece, for placemats; one 20"-square piece, for napkins; one 1½" x 20" piece, for decorative stripe

6 yards of 60"-wide cotton jersey, for placemat and napkin

1 yard of 60"-wide cotton jersey in different color, for decorative trim

Paper scissors

Garment scissors

Embroidery scissors

Rotary cutter and cutting mat

18" transparent plastic ruler

Tailor's chalk or disappearing-ink fabric pen

Hand-sewing needle

Button craft thread

Embroidery floss

Pins

1. Label Patterns

On the 14" x 20" piece of pattern paper, draw a straight line parallel to one of the paper's short sides, and label this line "Grain Line" and the entire pattern piece "Placemat."

On the 20"-square piece of pattern paper, draw a straight line parallel to any side, and label this line "Grain Line" and the entire pattern piece "Napkin."

On the 1½" x 20" piece of pattern paper, draw a straight line parallel to one of the short sides for this piece's grain line, and label the entire pattern piece "Decorative Stripe."

Labeling Patterns

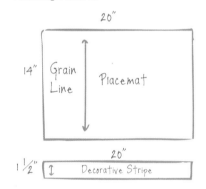
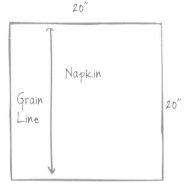

2. Cut Out Placemats and Napkins

Each placemat is made with three layers of cotton jersey and you can cut them out two layers at a time. Make sure when positioning the two layers that the grain line (see page 11) on each layer runs in the same direction. Then position your Placemat pattern piece on the two fabric layers so that the fabrics' and pattern's grain lines likewise run in the same direction.

Using tailor's chalk, trace around the pattern's edges. Remove the pattern and cut out two pieces at once, using your rotary cutter and cutting mat, and making sure to cut in a smooth line just inside the chalked line to remove it entirely. You now have two placemat pieces. Repeat the cutting process until you have a total of 18 pieces for six placemats.

Each napkin is made with a single layer of fabric. Using your Napkin pattern, repeat the cutting process to cut a total of six napkin pieces.

Each placemat and napkin uses four contrasting-color stripes, so you'll need 48 for six placemats and napkins. Using your Decorative Stripe pattern, repeat the cutting process to cut 48 decorative stripes from the contrasting color of cotton jersey.

3. Pin Placemats Together and Sew Two Edges

Align the placemat's top and two backing layers, right sides up, and pin the layers together. Using a straight stitch (see page 22), begin stitching the pinned pieces together ¼" from the raw edges on one short (14") side, starting at the top edge of the placemat. Wrap-stitch (see page 29) the beginning and end of the seam to secure it. As you sew, make sure to check your thread tension, so the fabric lies flat before you tie off the thread at the end of your seam. Repeat the above process on the placemat's other short side.

4. Add Eyelet Embroidery to Decorative Stripes

Align two of the constrasting-color stripes matching the grain lines, and pin them together. Using embroidery floss or thread and following the instructions on page 62, add eyelet embroidery to the decorative stripe, as pictured in the photo opposite, adding as much or as little embroidery as you like.

Repeat this process to make a total of 12 double-layer decorative stripes.

5. Attach Decorative Stripes to Placemats

Align one eyelet-embroidered decorative stripe over the placemat's long top edge and a second decorative stripe over its bottom edge, and pin the stripes in place. Using a straight stitch, begin stitching the decorative stripe to the placemat's top edge ¼" from the raw edges and closing the top edge of the placemat as you go. Wrap-stitch the beginning and end of the seam, and check your thread tension as you sew, as you did in Step 3. Then repeat the process to stitch the inner edge of the decorative stripe.

Repeat the process above to attach the decorative stripe to the placemat's bottom edge. Then repeat this step to attach the decorative stripes on the remaining five placemats.

6. Add Decorative Stripes to Napkins

Align one single-layer decorative stripe along all four edges of your napkin, overlapping the stripes at the corners, and pin them in place. Using a straight stitch, begin stitching each decorative stripe to the napkin ¼" from the raw edges starting at the top edge of the napkin. As you sew, make sure to check your thread tension, so the fabric lies flat before you knot off the thread at the end of your seam. Stitch continuously around all four edges securing your decorative stripes' outside edges to your napkin. Then repeat the process to attach the inner edges of the decorative stripes.

Repeat this step to attach decorative stripes to the remaining five napkins.

Stitching Decorative Stripes to Placemat and Napkin

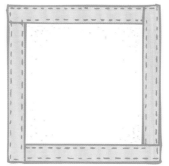

Placemat

Napkin

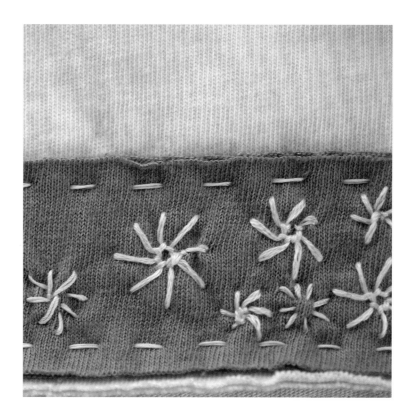

Alabama Studio Autumn Brunch

I love to throw a yearly autumn brunch sometime after the midsummer pickling party (see page 132) and before the holiday celebrations that begin in late November. This seasonal get-together has a long tradition in old-time quilting circles. Women didn't really have time to visit one another during the summer months, when there were gardens to tend, yards to mow, pickles and tomatoes to put up, and so much more. But as autumn progressed and the days shortened, they were freer to socialize around a quilting frame.

Menu

Alabama's Bloody Mary

Put-Up Tomato Tart

Warm Goat Cheese Salad with
Cider Vinegar Salad Dressing

Greens & Pot Likker

Cornbread or "Cornsticks"

Alabama's Bloody Mary
Serves 6–8

Nothing is quite as good as a Bloody Mary made from the juice of "put-up" tomatoes. And nothing gets a brunch started quite like this Alabama-style Mary.

3 cups tomato juice (use juice leftover from Put-Up Tomato Tart on page 136, if available)
1 cup vodka
4 teaspoons Worcestershire sauce
6–8 dashes Tabasco sauce (or to taste)
Juice of 2 limes
Salt and freshly ground pepper to taste
Olives, pickled okra, or Tomolives (pickled green cherry tomatoes; see page 137) for garnish

Stir all ingredients but the garnishes together in a serving pitcher and add ice. Thread the olives and pickles onto skewers and use to decorate individual glasses.

Put-Up Tomato Tart
Makes one 9" tart; serves 6–8

This tart is a riff on a church cookbook standard called Tomato Pie. Typically made in the summer with fresh tomatoes, this tart takes on a more robust personality when prepared with roasted tomatoes. It is also a good way to enjoy tomatoes out of season.

9" baked pie crust (at right)
20 ounces tomatoes (either home-canned or good-quality store-bought)
¼ cup extra-virgin olive oil
2 tablespoons fresh thyme
½ teaspoon salt
1 teaspoon freshly ground black pepper
¾ cup grated sharp cheese (such as cheddar, Parmesan, or our favorite Southern cheese for grating, Sweet Grass Dairy's Myrtlewood)
¾ cup mayonnaise (homemade or store-bought)
8 pieces bacon, crumbled (we recommend Benton's from Tennessee)
⅓ cup Ritz crackers broken into small, rough pieces about the size of a dime

Preheat oven to 350° F.

Drain the tomatoes, reserving the juice, and dice them into 1" pieces. In a medium bowl, combine the tomatoes, half the olive oil, the thyme, salt, and pepper, tossing with your hands until all of the tomatoes have a little oil on them. Pour the remaining olive oil onto a sheet pan, rubbing with your hands to coat the bottom of the pan, then spread the tomatoes in the pan in a single layer. Roast the tomatoes for about 15 minutes, until they start to dry and shrivel slightly.

In a small bowl, combine the grated cheese and mayonnaise; set aside.

Stir the cooked bacon into the tomatoes; then fill the baked pie crust ¾ full with this mixture. Spread the cheese-mayo mixture over the tomato mixture. Sprinkle the crushed crackers over the top. Bake for 30 minutes, until the tart is bubbly and starts to brown slightly on top. Serve warm or at room temperature.

Pie Crust
Makes one 9" pie or tart crust or 3" tartlets

1 cup all-purpose flour
¼ teaspoon salt
¼ cup salted butter or shortening
Up to ¼ cup cold water

Preheat oven to 425° F.

Combine flour and salt in a bowl or food processor bowl. Add shortening and, with the knife blade, or by hand using a pastry cutter or two butter knives, blend until dough resembles coarse oatmeal. Slowly add the cold water, 1 tablespoon at a time, until the dough leaves the sides of the bowl and forms a ball. Remove the dough ball, flatten slightly to form a thick disk, and cover completely in an airtight container or in plastic wrap so that dough does not dry out while chilling. Chill for at least 30 minutes.

Roll the chilled dough to about ⅛" thickness in one round shape to fit into a 9" pie pan or in twelve round shapes to fit into a standard muffin pan. Gently press the dough into the pie pan or muffin pan, being careful not to make a hole. Trim any excess from around the edges and fold the edges under. If desired, make a decorative fluted edge or press all around with the tines of a fork to make a pattern. Prick the bottom of the crust with a fork to allow trapped air to escape during the baking process and to keep the dough from bubbling up. Bake for about 8 minutes, or until the crust is a light, golden brown.

Warm Goat Cheese Salad
Serves 6–8

This hearty salad combines autumn greens and goat cheese. In northwest Alabama, we are lucky to have an excellent fresh goat-cheese maker called Belle Chèvre. Look around at your local farmers' market for great cheeses from your region.

2 cups dry, fine, toasted bread crumbs
2 teaspoons herbes de Provence or ground black pepper
Goat cheese log, approximately 8 to 10 ounces
½ cup extra-virgin olive oil
6–8 handfuls mixed lettuces and greens
Cider Vinegar Salad Dressing (at right)
Parchment paper

Line a baking sheet with parchment paper. Mix the bread crumbs with the herbs or pepper, and place in a plate or shallow bowl. Cut the goat cheese crosswise into eight equal pieces to form eight little patties. With lightly oiled hands (use olive oil), dip the patties into the olive oil and then the bread crumbs, coating each piece evenly. Place on the prepared baking sheet. Place in the refrigerator for at least 20 minutes and up to 24 hours before baking.

Preheat the oven to 375°F. Transfer the baking sheet with the goat cheese directly from the refrigerator to the oven. Bake for about 10 minutes, or until the crumbs start to brown and the cheese begins to melt.

Toss the greens with just enough Cider Vinegar Salad Dressing to coat and divide among plates. Place rounds of cheese on top of or to the side of the salad.

Cider Vinegar Salad Dressing
Makes about ½ cup dressing

The tangy aroma of this old-time Southern dressing reminds me of my childhood.

¼ cup cider vinegar
2 tablespoons sugar
1 teaspoon salt
¼ teaspoon freshly ground black pepper
2 tablespoons extra-virgin olive oil

In a glass jar with a tight-fitting lid, combine the cider vinegar, sugar, salt, and pepper, and shake well to combine until the sugar dissolves. Add the oil and shake very hard to emulsify. You can store this dressing in a cool place for up to 2 weeks.

Greens & Pot Likker
Serves 8

This classic Southern, poor-folk food is just about the best thing to warm you up on cool autumn days. *Pot likker* refers to the liquid, or "liquor," that is left in the pot after the greens are cooked. This dish is traditionally served with a side of cornbread. For parties and special occasions, serve in your best china teacups.

4 slices of good, smoked bacon, diced (optional)

4 tablespoons vegetable oil or olive oil (if not using bacon)

1 medium onion, diced

2 cloves garlic, minced

1 teaspoon red pepper flakes, or 1 teaspoon seeded and minced jalapeño or serrano pepper

3 large bunches collard, turnip, or mustard greens (or any combination), washed, stemmed, and roughly torn or chopped into 3" pieces

1 teaspoon salt

1 tablespoon sugar

In a medium-sized saucepan, heat 8 cups water over medium-high heat to keep it hot but not boiling.

In a large stockpot, slowly brown bacon for about 8 minutes. Remove from the pan and set aside, keeping the rendered fat in the bottom of the pan. (If not using bacon fat, use the oil.) Heat the bacon fat or oil, then add onion and allow to sweat for about 2 minutes. Add garlic and stir with a wooden spoon, being careful not to brown. Add the red pepper flakes or fresh pepper and then the greens in two or three batches. The greens will take up lots of room in the pot to begin with, but as you turn them over in the hot grease, they will begin to wilt.

Keep turning and adding fresh greens until they are all slightly coated in the oil and wilted. Be careful not to allow them to stick to the bottom of the pan. The greens will pop and sizzle as they release their liquid. Sprinkle in the salt and sugar, and continue turning the greens in the oil until they are all wilted and dark green. Add the warm stock to the pot, stir, and cover. Reduce the heat to low, and simmer for 45 minutes to an hour. Serve the greens and some of the liquid in soup bowls with cornbread (see opposite).

Cornbread or "Cornsticks"
Makes one 9" round or 12 cornsticks

There is nothing more delicious than a cornbread muffin to dip into your pot likker. I like to make my muffins in a cast-iron pan with openings that look like little ears of corn, otherwise known as a cornstick pan.

½ cup rendered bacon fat, butter, vegetable shortening, or vegetable oil (or a combination)
2 cups yellow cornmeal
½ cup all-purpose flour
1 teaspoon baking powder
1 teaspoon baking soda
¾ teaspoon salt
1½ cups buttermilk
1 large egg, lightly beaten

Preheat oven to 450° F. Distribute bacon fat or other grease among 12 individual cups of a cornstick pan or put in a 9" cast-iron skillet, and place in the hot oven to melt and heat up—about 5 minutes.

While the pan is heating, in a large bowl, mix cornmeal and flour with baking powder, baking soda, and salt. Slowly add buttermilk, and mix just to combine. When grease is hot, carefully remove it from oven, and pour all but about 2 teaspoons of it into flour mixture. Stir the grease into batter, add egg, and stir to combine. Do not mix this too vigorously, or the bread will be tough.

Pour the mixture into the prepared hot pan, and place in the oven to bake until golden brown, with a crispy crust along the sides—about 25 minutes for cornbread and 15 minutes for cornsticks. Remove from oven, flip bread or cornsticks out onto a plate, and serve warm with butter.

Woven Farm Chairs (or Friendship Chairs)

While on an extended visit to my home in Florence, my dear friend and colleague Eva Whitechapel spotted a few old chairs with broken seats and decided to repair them using cotton-jersey pulls made from fabric scraps. Later, my partner, folk artist Butch Anthony, expanded upon Eva's idea, reweaving the seats and also decorating the chairs in different ways, such as painting, stenciling, or carving inspirational words and sayings or important dates into the wood. And now they are part of our home collection. Because two friends brought this project to life, I like to call these Friendship Chairs. I complete many of the Friendship Chairs in my home with Relief Appliqué Chair Pillows (see page 153).

Our Design Choices

Chair — **Light green**

Cotton-jersey pulls — **White and light green**

Supplies

Ladder-back chair, with seat removed

About 44 yards of cotton-jersey pulls (see page 99), each pull at least 1½" wide before pulling and 8" longer than chair seat's width

Large crochet hook (size D or larger)

Garment scissors, for cutting pulls and trimming after weaving

Additional Supplies

Note: Additional supplies needed will depend on the condition of your chair and what kind of decoration you want to add. Following are some possibilities:

VOC-free paint (without volatile organic chemicals)

Paintbrush

Stencil

Metal wire (we use 17-gauge electric-fence aluminum wire)

Wood carving tool (such as a craft knife, utility knife, pocket knife, or Dremel)

Needle-nose pliers with wire cutter

Hammer

4-penny finishing nails

Jute twine

Leather shoe strings or ropes

1. Choose Chair and Repair If Needed

If you're handy, it's fine to choose chairs that need repair. If you're not, start with stable chairs.

We gather our chairs from thrift and antique stores, friends, neighbors, and even the side of the road, so they are often old, delicate, and unstable. Butch takes them apart and, using wood glue, metal wire, and sometimes leather shoe strings or ropes, puts them back together again. If the chair we've chosen is rickety, he stabilizes it by cross-wiring the legs using wire, cotton-jersey pulls, or twine (see photo at left).

2. Decorate Chair

To decorate the chair's back, seat, legs, or arms, we favor painting, stenciling, and carving. When painting, we use standard VOC-free house paint applied with a paintbrush. Sometimes we paint a stencil on a chair back and/or carve words or special dates into the back of the chair.

3. Prepare Cotton-Jersey Pulls

So that your woven chair seat will be strong and durable for generations, we recommend cutting your cotton-jersey strips at least 1½" wide (measured before pulling them, a process described on page 99). Usually we just mix up the cotton-jersey scraps on hand, selecting colors to create a pleasing pattern. But I also like to cut pulls in one color family and then add one startlingly different color as an accent.

4. Prepare Seat's Warp

In weaving, a series of warp threads is first attached to the loom from front to back, and then weft threads are woven side to side through the warp threads to create the fabric. In this project, the chair's seat frame serves as your loom, and a warp is made out of cotton-jersey pulls, as follows: Starting at the front rung of the chair on the far left or right, make a double knot (see right), leaving a tail. Position this and all knots on the bottom of the chair rail (see photo). Working from one side of the chair to the other, wrap a cotton-jersey pull tautly (but not tightly) around the front and back rails to create parallel rows, leaving about ½" to ¾" between each row. Continue until you reach the opposite side of the chair, attaching new cotton-jersey pulls and using a double knot as necessary on the front or back rails. Our double-knot method calls for leaving approximately 6" at the beginning or end of each cotton-jersey pull, which creates "fringe." If you want a fringe in a spot on the rail that's wrapped but not knotted, simply tie on a short cotton-jersey pull at that point.

Tying Pull to Rung Using Double Knot

Leave about 6" free at end of your cotton-jersey pull; then wrap pull around front seat rail once or twice, pulling strip taut. Bring strip back up to top of rail, pass it over warp "thread," bring it back under warp thread, and pull it through loop you just made.

5. Weave Seat's Weft

To complete the chair seat, weave cotton-jersey-pull weft threads under and over the warp threads that you just attached as follows: Double-knot your first cotton jersey pull at one end of a warp rail (that is, one of the chair's two side rails), then weave the weft strip over one warp strip and under the next, repeating this process until you've crossed the entire seat. Knot off at the end of the warp row, or, if your cotton-jersey pull is long enough to weave back across the seat, do so and knot off on the warp rung where you started, leaving extra length for fringe, as in Step 4. Once you've woven the first two rows, the rest will be easy.

If necessary, use a crochet hook large enough for your cotton-jersey pulls to pull the warp strips through tight places and for packing the strips into the warp. Follow the directions in Step 4 for ending your pull-strips and double-knotting them to finish.

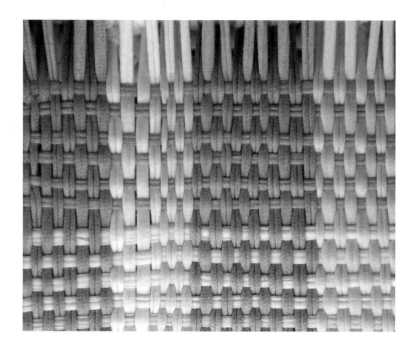

Weaving Seat

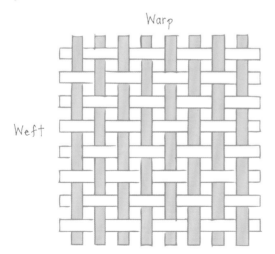

6. Tie Knots at End of Fringe and Trim Fringe

I like to tie knots on the ends of my fringe warp and weft strips, and I vary the pattern in every chair. After tying a simple overhand knot (see the drawing below) at a uniform point on each strip, I trim the fringe just below the knot. To get the look in the photograph on page 96, don't knot and cut all the strips to one level; instead stagger the knots and cut lengths irregularly.

Overhand Knot for End of Fringe

Cotton-Jersey Pulls

When cotton-jersey fabric is cut across, or against, the grain line (see page 11), its cut edge will roll to the fabric's right side; and, conversely, when the fabric is cut with the grain line, its cut edge will roll to the wrong side. We use this fabric trait to create small "ropes" of cotton jersey from fabric scraps, which we try to reuse in new projects, such as the seats for the Woven Farm Chairs and for innumerable other purposes—to close and tie wrap shirts, tie packages, hold down furniture when moving, secure tomato plants to their stakes in the garden, and hold bookshelves against walls. I also use them to hold back my hair.

We call these handy devices cotton-jersey "pulls" because of the way you make them: Simply cut your cotton-jersey scraps into strips from 1" to 3" wide, depending on the thickness desired. You may choose to cut them with or against the grain to control which way the strip's edges curl. After a strip is cut, grab one end in each hand, and pull. That's it!

Eyelet-Embroidered Gore Skirt

I've never met a woman who likes everything about her body. One doesn't like her legs; another doesn't like her backside. Now, I've been a "womanly" woman ever since I developed the shapes and curves that tend to define that term. And while I love my shapely figure, I don't necessarily like clothing that shows off every curve. This skirt is the perfect solution. Neither too tight nor too wide, it's feminine and easy to pull on, looks great on lots of different figures, and can be worn for just about any occasion.

Our Design Choices

Fabric — **Blue**

Thread — **Blue for construction**
Grey for embroidery

Embroidery floss — **Light and dark grey**

Stretch stitch — **Herringbone**

Felling stitch — **Parallel whipstitch**

Seams — **Open-felled on right side**

Knots — **Inside garment**

Bugle beads — **Grey**

Fold-over elastic — **Blue**

Supplies

Gore Skirt pattern (see pattern sheet at back of book)

4 yards of 60"-wide cotton-jersey fabric

1 yard of $1\frac{1}{2}$"-wide fold-over elastic

Paper scissors

Garment scissors

Rotary cutter and cutting mat

18" transparent plastic ruler

Tailor's chalk or disappearing-ink fabric pen

Hand-sewing needle

Button craft thread

All-purpose sewing thread

Embroidery floss

Pins

Approximately 325 bugle beads

1. Prepare and Cut Pattern

Photocopy or trace the Gore Skirt pattern, and use your paper scissors to cut the traced or photocopied pattern in your desired size (see page 37), cutting as close as possible to the black cutting lines. Note that the Center Front and Center Back pattern pieces are half-patterns, which are meant to be cut on the folded fabric, with the pattern edge marked "Place on fold" positioned accordingly. Note, too, that all the pattern pieces have a ¼" seam allowance built into the edges, except for the waistline and hem edges, which, for this skirt, are left raw and, in the case of the waistline, bound.

The Gore Skirt pattern has a total of six pattern pieces: 1 Center Front, 2 Side Fronts, 1 Center Back, and 2 Side Backs.

You'll cut two fabric pieces for each pattern piece—a top layer and a backing layer—and you can cut these two pieces at the same time by layering two pieces of the cotton jersey right side up. Make sure when positioning the two layers that the fabric's grain line (see page 11) on each layer runs in the same direction. Likewise be sure to position the pattern piece on the two layers so that the fabrics' and pattern's grain lines run in the same direction.

Using tailor's chalk, trace around the pattern's edges. Then remove the pattern, and cut out the two pieces at once, using your rotary cutter and cutting mat, and making sure to cut in a smooth line just inside the chalked line so that you remove it entirely.

When finished, you will have a total of 12 cut-fabric pattern pieces.

2. Pin Pattern's Top and Backing Layers

Align each top-layer pattern piece on each corresponding backing-layer piece, with both fabrics facing right side up, and pat the layers into place so that their edges are aligned. Securely pin together the edges of both layers on each piece.

3. Stitch Eyelet Embroidery

Following the instructions for eyelet embroidery starting on page 62, embroider eyelets randomly along the skirt's hemline, fading to no embroidery about 7" from the hemline. Use the detail photograph opposite to help you decide on the embroidery's placement. You may want to space the eyelets very close together or further apart. You might also decide to continue adding embellishments over time.

4. Assemble Front and Back Pieces

With the fabric wrong sides together and the cut edges aligned, pin one Side Front piece to each side of the Center Front piece. Following the instructions for sewing floating seams on the right side on page 27 and using a straight stitch (see page 22), begin sewing the pinned pieces together ¼" from the raw edges, starting at the skirt's top edge. Wrap-stitch (see page 29) the beginning and end of every seam to secure it. As you sew, make sure to check your thread tension, so the fabric lies flat before you tie off the thread at the end of your seam.

After assembling the skirt's front, carefully iron each seam's allowances open. Then finish the seams by following the instructions for sewing an open-felled seam on the right side on page 29, using a parallel whipstitch (see page 25), stitching from the bottom to the top of the skirt's front, and wrap-stitching the beginning and end of every seam to secure it. Your resulting seams will be visible on the garment's right side.

Repeat the process above to join the three pieces of the Gore Skirt's back, stitching one Side Back panel to each side of the Center Back panel.

5. Assemble Gore Skirt

With wrong sides together and the edges aligned, pin the Gore Skirt's completed front and back panels together. Then sew the seams just as you did in Step 4.

6. Bind Waistline

Using 1½"-wide fold-over elastic and starting at the skirt's center-back waistline, encase the waistline's raw edge with the folded elastic, and pin it in place. Overlap the elastic's raw edges at the center back by about ½", and trim any excess elastic. Using the stretch stitch of your choice (see page 24), sew through all the layers down the middle of the elastic.

Angie's Fall Scarf

We originally designed this scarf for our Fall/Winter 2008 Revolution Collection, which was inspired by photographer Charles Moore's stirring images of the Civil Rights movement in Alabama. The catalog for that collection was a beautiful mixture of historical documents, photographs of the New South, and recipes for change. When designing these pieces, we thought of the work as a celebration of the men, women, and children who stood, walked, and sang together to make this nation a better place. I love this scarf; it is small and easy to work on and is loved by everyone, male and female, young and old.

Our Design Choices

Top fabric — **Natural**

Backing fabric — **Black**

Stencil — **Angie's Fall**

Paint — **Washed-black**

Embroidery floss — **Taupe**

Thread — **Cream**

Seams — **Felled on wrong side**

Knots — **Inside scarf**

Supplies

One 7" x 38" rectangle and one 7" x 6" rectangle of pattern paper or butcher paper (see page 14)

¼ yard of 60"-wide cotton jersey in each of two colors

Angie's Fall stencil (see page 31)

Textile paint

Tools for your choice of stencil-transfer method (see page 42)

Garment scissors

Embroidery scissors

18" transparent plastic ruler

Tailor's chalk or disappearing-ink fabric pen

Hand-sewing needle

Button craft thread

Embroidery floss

Pins

1. Label Pattern

On your 7" x 38" rectangle of pattern paper, draw a line parallel to one short side, and label the line "Grain Line," and the entire pattern piece "Scarf Piece."

Labeling Pattern

2. Cut Out Scarf Pattern

Lay the fabric for the scarf's top, layer right side up, and place the Scarf Piece pattern on top of the fabric, making sure that the pattern's marked grain line and the fabric's grain line (see page 11) run in the same direction. With tailor's chalk, carefully trace around the pattern's edges. Then remove the pattern and cut out the piece, making sure to cut in a smooth line just inside the chalked line to remove it entirely.

Now lay the fabric for the scarf's backing layer right side up, and place the scarf's top layer on it, making sure that the grain lines of the two fabrics run in the same direction. Carefully cut the backing fabric layer around the edge of the top layer, so that you have a duplicate backing piece. (Using the cut fabric pattern piece as the pattern rather than the paper pattern piece itself automatically adds $1/16$" extra on the piece you're cutting, which is exactly the extra amount we like to add to a backing layer to get the best results with reverse appliqué.)

3. Stencil Design on Pattern Pieces

Lay the scarf's top layer right side up on a prepared work surface (see page 42). Place the Angie's Fall stencil on top of it, positioning it at one end. Using textile paint and the washed-black stenciling method (see page 46), as we did, or the textile paint-transfer method of your choice (see page 44), carefully transfer the stencil design onto the pattern piece and let the paint dry to the touch. Reposition the stencil and repeat the transfer process to stencil the scarf's entire top layer. Allow the stenciled design to dry thoroughly.

4. Backstitch Reverse Appliqué Angie's Fall Pattern

Align the scarf's top layer over the backing layer, both right sides up. Following the instructions for backstitched reverse appliqué on page 54, backstitch around the edge of each element of the stenciled Angie's Fall design on the scarf's top layer. Cut away the top layer of fabric within the medium and large elements of the stitched design to reveal the backing layer beneath, and leave the small elements backstitched but uncut.

5. Make Fringe

Cut four 7" x 6" rectangles from the fabric scraps that you used for the scarf's top layer. Align two rectangles, both right side up with the grain lines running in the same direction, and stitch the pair as a unit to one end of the scarf with right sides together, so the seam shows on the scarf's wrong side. Then fell the seam allowance (see page 28) towards what will become the fringe, using a straight stitch (see page 22) and beginning and ending with wrap-stitches (see page 29) to secure these felled seams. Use your garment scissors to cut fringe on this scarf end, slashing the fabric to $1/8$" from the seam line every $1/4$".

Repeat the process above with the remaining two cut rectangles to create fringe on the scarf's other end.

Market Bags

Over the last few years, the bag has become the fashion accessory of choice (although, personally, I still favor the shoe). There are endless patterns for fabric bags on the market and most of them can be made using cotton jersey and the embellishment techniques presented in this book.

Making a bag can be as easy as cutting a large rectangle, folding it in half, sewing the side seams and adding a strap. For the bags shown here, I combined 12" x 14" fronts and backs with a 2" -wide side/bottom panel that extends all the way around and 14" long straps. I did everything in double layers for strength and then added a lining so that the stitches and knots are hidden on the inside. For both bags, I used the Angie's Fall stencil. For the one on the right, I colored and stenciled the fabric with our Faded Leaves technique (see page 49) and then traced the flowers with a black Sharpie marker; for the bag on the left, I transferred the Angie's Fall pattern with washed-black stenciling (see page 46), added piping where the front and back attach to the sides, and then worked backstitched reverse appliqué (see page 54) with embroidery floss around all of the shapes.

I have made quite a few of these bags and really enjoy embellishing each one a little differently. I use them for all sorts of purposes, from grocery-shopping to transporting my laptop from home to office, to storing my daughter's school supplies.

Medallion Boudoir Pillow

The Medallion Boudoir Pillow is a small, rectangular decorative throw pillow that can be made in any size you want. We've made this pillow as small as 6" x 10" and as large as the width of a standard double bed. Whatever their size, these pillows make great accents for a couch, chair, or bed. I love them in simple color-blocked versions and, as we've done here, with the front side embellished with backstitched reverse appliqué.

Our Design Choices

Front top fabric — **Carmine red**

Front backing fabric — **Faded Leaves**

Back fabric — **Carmine red**

Piping — **Natural (wet-paint stenciled in Faded Leaves color)**

Stencil — **Large Medallion**

Paint — **Burgundy**

Thread — **Red**

Knots — **Inside pillow**

Supplies

One 12" x 20" rectangle and one 12" square of pattern paper or butcher paper (see page 14)

¾ yard of 60"-wide cotton jersey, for front top and back

½ yard of 60"-wide natural cotton jersey, for front backing and piping

Supplies for Faded Leaves stenciling (see page 48)

Angie's Fall stencil (see page 31)

Large Medallion stencil (see page 66)

Textile paint

One pair each of garment and embroidery scissors

Rotary cutter and cutting mat

18" transparent plastic ruler

Tailor's chalk or disappearing-ink fabric pen

Hand-sewing needle

Button craft thread

Pins

12" x 20" pillow form

1. Label Patterns

Using a pencil and ruler, draw a line parallel to the 12" side of the rectangle of pattern paper or butcher paper. Label the line "Grain Line" and the square itself "Boudoir Pillow Front."

On the 12" square of pattern paper, draw a line parallel to any side, and label it "Grain Line" and the square itself "Boudoir Pillow Back."

Labeling Patterns

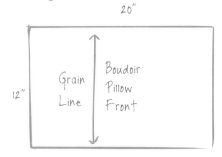 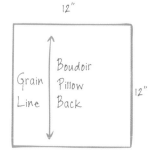

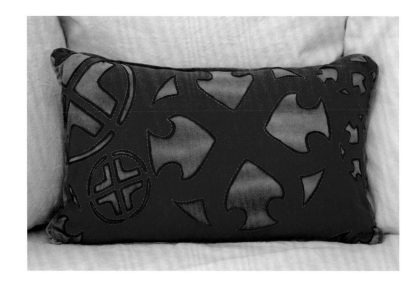

2. Cut Out Pillow Front and Back

Cut the fabric for the pillow back's top and bottom layers in half widthwise, and layer the two pieces right side up, making sure that the grain line (see page 11) on both pieces runs in the same direction. Place the Boudoir Pillow Back pattern on top of the two aligned layers, again matching the direction of the pattern's marked grain line with the fabrics' grain lines.

Using tailor's chalk, trace around the pattern's edges. Then remove the pattern, and cut out two pieces at once, using your rotary cutter and cutting mat, and making sure to cut in a smooth line just inside the chalked line so that you remove it entirely. You now have two pillow-back pieces.

Reposition your pattern piece on the remainder of the two fabric layers, and repeat the cutting process so that you have a total of four pillow-back pieces.

Next lay out a single layer of the fabric, right side up, that you want to use for the pillow front's top layer. Place the Boudoir Pillow Front pattern on the fabric, making sure the pattern's and fabric's grain lines run in the same direction. Trace and cut out the pattern.

Finally, lay out a single layer of the fabric, right side up, that you want to use for the pillow-front's backing layer. Place the Boudoir Pillow Front pattern on this fabric, again aligning the pattern's and fabric's grain lines. Trace and cut out the pattern.

When finished, you'll have four fabric Boudoir Pillow Back pieces in the same color and two fabric Boudoir Pillow Fronts in different colors.

3. Color Backing Fabric for Front with Faded Leaves

Following the directions on page 48, wet-paint stencil the pillow front's backing fabric using the Angie's Fall stencil and black paint to create the Faded Leaves effect on the fabric.

4. Stencil Design on Pattern Pieces

Lay the cut pattern piece for the pillow-front's top layer, right side up on your stenciling work surface (see page 42). Place the Large Medallion stencil on top of the pillow front piece. Then, using textile paint and your stencil-transfer method of choice, carefully transfer the stencil design onto the pattern piece. Allow the stenciled design to dry thoroughly.

5. Backstitch Reverse Appliqué Medallion Pattern

Following the instructions for backstitched reverse appliqué on page 54, align the pillow front's top and backing layers, right sides up and with the grain line running in the same directions. Backstitch around the stenciled Medallion design on the pillow front. Then cut away the top layer of fabric to reveal the backing layer beneath.

6. Fold and Stitch Edges of Pillow Backs

To construct the pillow's back, follow the directions in Step 6 of the String-Quilted Pillow on page 75.

7. Prepare and Pin Piping to Pillow Front

To cut, prepare, and pin piping strips on the follow front, follow the directions in Step 7 of the String-Quilted Pillow.

8. Pin and Stitch Front to Backs

To pin and stitch the pillow's front and backs together, follow the directions in Step 8 of the String-Quilted Pillow. Then turn your pillow case right side out, and slip your pillow into the case.

Felted Wool Appliqués

To add more layers or texture to your pillow or any other project (as we did for the grey and black pillow shown here), consider making your own felt appliqué shapes out of vintage wool. Old coats and even the ugliest wool skirt you find thrifting can be transformed into a beautiful fabric by felting it.

To make felt, wash your wool items in the washing machine in hot water for a full cycle. Lay the items flat to dry or, if you want a thicker, more condensed felt, wash again and/or throw them into the dryer.

Cut the dried felt into the desired shape. Because felting shrinks the fabric and locks the wool fibers together, fraying should be minimal; if you see a few stray threads, trim them.

Alabama Studio Celebration

This great menu is easy and delicious, and celebrates the nostalgic tastes and tables of Southern grandmothers. The quantities are large to satisfy a big celebration for a hungry family; simply cut the recipes in half for smaller gatherings. I was once asked how we say "Bon appétit" in my native South and my answer was "Dig in."

Menu

Pan-Fried Chicken

Cheese Grits Casserole

Deviled Eggs

Angie's Classic Cupcakes

Pan-Fried Chicken
Serves 12–15

Fried chicken should be on every party menu. It is incredibly delicious, keeps well for several hours, and reminds me of the best of the South. Although it takes time and care to get it right, this recipe is foolproof.

12–15 mixed pieces of chicken, with skin on
½ gallon buttermilk
1½ cups all-purpose flour
2 teaspoons salt
1 teaspoon freshly ground black pepper
½ teaspoon cayenne pepper
Vegetable oil, for frying

Rinse the chicken pieces, and shake them to remove excess water. Place in a container with a lid, add buttermilk to cover, seal, and refrigerate for at least 1 hour or overnight. Mix flour, salt, and black and cayenne peppers in a shallow bowl. Drain the buttermilk and leave the chicken in its bowl.

Heat 1" oil in a deep cast-iron skillet over medium-high heat until water sprinkled into the oil pops or the oil reaches about 350° F. Dredge the chicken in the flour mixture, coating the entire surface, and gently lay it into the hot oil. Do not crowd the pieces in the skillet! You will have to do 2 or 3 batches (maybe more). Fry each piece for about 10 minutes. (Very thick thighs or breasts may need a couple of minutes more.) Turn once, being careful not to knock off the coating, and cook for another 10 minutes or until a meat thermometer reads 165° F.

Transfer chicken to a baking rack placed over a pan to catch any excess grease. Allow to rest for at least 10 minutes before serving.

Cheese Grits Casserole
Serves 12–15

This hearty casserole is a favorite Southern side dish to go with fried chicken. It's easy and inexpensive to make for a crowd and really is Southern comfort food at its finest!

2 cups grits (do not use instant or quick grits)
1 tablespoon salt
½ cup unsalted butter
1 teaspoon freshly ground black pepper
1½ cups shredded sharp cheddar cheese
3 large eggs, beaten

Preheat oven to 350° F.

In a large saucepan, combine 8 cups water with the grits and salt, and bring to a boil, stirring often. Cook for approximately 10 minutes or until the grits are thick and creamy, but not lumpy or approaching a solid state.

Stir in the butter, pepper, and cheese. Allow to cool for a couple of minutes, then stir in the eggs. Pour the entire mixture into a greased, ovenproof, 9" x13" baking dish, and cook for 30 to 40 minutes, or until firm and golden brown on top.

Deviled Eggs
Serves 12–15

Deviled eggs are a fun party appetizer. It is a Southern tradition for mothers to pass down to their daughters the dish on which they serve deviled eggs.

12 hard-boiled eggs (see Note)
½ cup mayonnaise (homemade, if you can)
2 teaspoons Dijon mustard
½ teaspoon salt, or to taste
½ teaspoon freshly ground black pepper, or to taste
2 dashes of hot sauce
3 tablespoons sweet pickle relish (optional)
Green onion or paprika, for garnish

Note: My grandmother swore by the "boil and rest" method of boiling eggs: In a saucepan, cover eggs with cold water, and add 2 tablespoons salt. Bring water to a boil, remove from heat, cover, and let "rest" for 10 minutes. Pour off hot water, cover with cold water, replace the lid, and let "rest" for another 20 minutes. Peel and cool the eggs.

Slice the boiled eggs in half lengthwise, and transfer yolks to a mixing bowl, being careful not to tear the whites. Set the whites aside on an egg plate or other serving dish, hole side up. Mash the yolks with a fork until very fine. Add the mayonnaise, mustard, salt, pepper, and hot sauce, mixing well until smooth and creamy. Stir in the relish, if using. Spoon or pipe the yolk mixture back into the egg white "cups" and garnish. Keep eggs cool and covered with plastic wrap until ready to serve.

Angie's Classic Cupcakes
Makes 24 cupcakes

These classic yellow cupcakes with buttercream icing are topped with sweetened, shredded coconut. If you don't love coconut, use chocolate or rainbow sprinkles instead.

2 cups all-purpose flour
1 tablespoon baking powder
1 teaspoon salt
½ cup unsalted butter, softened
1¼ cups granulated sugar
2 large eggs
¾ cup milk
1 teaspoon pure vanilla extract
Easy Buttercream Icing (at right)
2 cups sweetened, shredded coconut, for topping cupcakes
12 cupcake liners

Preheat oven to 350° F.

Fill the muffin tins with cupcake liners. In a large mixing bowl, using a whisk or fork, combine the flour, baking powder, and salt. Set aside.

In the bowl of an electric mixer, cream the butter and sugar until it is light and fluffy (about 3 minutes). Add the eggs, one at a time, beating well after each addition. Next add one-third of the flour mixture and one-third of the milk, beating just enough to incorporate. Scrape down the sides of the bowl and add the next third of the dry and then the wet ingredients. Repeat to incorporate the rest of the flour mixture and milk, making sure not to over-mix. Scrape down the sides of the bowl one last time, add the vanilla, and beat just until everything is combined and smooth.

Pour the batter into the prepared cupcake liners, and bake for 15 to 20 minutes, or until the cake's center springs back when pressed lightly.

Turn the cupcakes out on cooling racks to cool completely before icing and sprinkling with coconut.

Easy Buttercream Icing

1 cup unsalted butter, softened
1 teaspoon pure vanilla extract
1 pound 10X powdered sugar
1–3 tablespoons milk, half-and-half, or cream

In the bowl of an electric mixer, cream the butter and vanilla until smooth. Gradually add the sugar, allowing the butter and sugar to cream together before adding more, scraping down the sides of the bowl as you go. The mixture should look a little dry at this point. Add the milk, 1 tablespoon at a time, beating on high speed until the icing is smooth and spreadable.

Sewing, Cooking, and Community

Cooking and community are permanently linked, especially within the Southern cultural landscape. The quilting bee of the early 20th century is a perfect example of this connection. Women often labored throughout the spring and summer planting and harvesting and then spent autumn stocking root cellars and readying their homes for the coming winter. Once this work was complete, they would gather—first in one home, then another—to stitch the quilts each family needed to get through the cold weather, all the while sharing family tales, as well as favorite and newly discovered recipes. My grandmother once told me that she looked forward to late autumn because that was when she could sit with her friends over a quilt. I've even heard that some ladies had recipes that they saved just for such occasions and that certain hostesses were favored for their delicious dishes.

It is this relationship between textiles, food, and community that bonded a friendship between stylist, writer, and Southern food historian Angie Mosier and me, and led us to create our Sewing, Cooking, and Community workshops, which we offer locally and across America. In these workshops, I teach one group the sewing techniques we use for our couture garments and answer questions about our business model and how participants can take what they are learning back to their own communities. At the same time, Angie teaches a second

group how to craft beautiful Southern meals from scratch and explains the history of the dishes they are preparing. We meet at mealtime. By the end of the weekend, friendships have been forged, problems have been worked through, skills have been learned, and stories have been shared—much as they were during the quilting bees of yesteryear.

Inked & Quilted Camisole Dress

I once had the opportunity to tour the costume collection at The Metropolitan Museum of Art in New York City. What a treat to see row after row of dresses from the 18th century hanging together—the richness, color, and bold patterns with subtle details seemed so modern to me. This dress project pays homage to that beautiful collection. It uses a simple technique that works up quickly but has a strong impact. I've turned the seams to the right side to show the structure of the dress and highlight the important curves.

Our Design Choices

Top fabric— **Natural**

Backing fabric — **Natural**

Binding fabric — **Natural**

Stencil — **Angie's Fall**

Paint — **Grey**

Marker — **Black**

Thread — **Navy for quilting**
Cream for construction

Stretch stitch — **Herringbone**

Seams — **Floating on right side**

Knots — **Outside garment**

Supplies

Camisole Dress pattern (see pattern sheet at back of book)

6 yards of 60"-wide cotton-jersey fabric

Angie's Fall stencil (see page 31)

Textile paint

Tools for your choice of stencil-transfer method (see page 42)

Sharpie marker, extra-fine

Paper scissors

Garment scissors

Rotary cutter and cutting mat

18" transparent plastic ruler

Tailor's chalk or disappearing-ink fabric pen

Hand-sewing needle

Button craft thread

All-purpose sewing thread

Pins

1. Prepare and Cut Pattern

Photocopy or trace the Camisole Dress pattern, and use your paper scissors to cut the photocopied or traced pattern in your desired size (see page 37), cutting as close as possible to the black cutting lines. Note that the Center Front and Center Back pattern pieces are half-patterns, which are meant to be cut on folded fabric with the pattern edge marked "Place on fold" positioned accordingly. Note, too, that all the pattern pieces have a ¼" seam allowance built into the edges, except for the neckline, armhole, and hem edges, which, for this dress, are left raw, with the neckline and armholes then bound.

The Camisole Dress has a total of six pattern pieces: 1 Center Front, 2 Side Fronts, 1 Center Back, and 2 Side Backs.

You'll cut two fabric pieces for each pattern piece—a top layer and a backing layer—and you can cut these two pieces at the same time by layering two pieces of the cotton jersey right side up. Make sure when positioning the two layers that the grain line (see page 11) on each layer runs in the same direction. Likewise be sure to position the pattern piece on the two layers so that the fabrics' and pattern's grain lines run in the same direction.

Using tailor's chalk, trace around the pattern's edges. Then remove the pattern, and cut out the two pieces at once, using your rotary cutter and cutting mat, and making sure to cut in a smooth line just inside the chalked line so that you remove it entirely.

When finished, you will have a total of 12 cut-fabric pattern pieces.

2. Baste Neck and Armholes

Using a single strand of all-purpose thread, baste (see page 22) all the neckline and armhole edges on the cut-fabric pieces, as indicated on the patterns, to prevent these edges from stretching while you're working on your Camisole Dress.

3. Stencil Design on Pattern Pieces

Arrange the top layer of the Camisole Dress's three front-pattern pieces right side up, placing each piece adjacent to its neighboring piece. Place the Angie's Fall stencil on one of the two Side Front pieces. Using textile paint and the textile-paint-transfer method of your choice, transfer the stencil design, and let the paint dry to the touch. Reposition the stencil to an adjacent area, and transfer the pattern again, repeating the process until you've painted an allover pattern on all the pattern pieces. Repeat the process for the three back-pattern pieces, and let all the stenciled designs dry thoroughly.

Stencil Adjacent Pattern Pieces

4. Ink Outline of Angie's Fall Design

Following the instructions for Inked & Quilted on page 56, use your Sharpie marker to trace around the outline of all the stenciled shapes in the Angie's Fall design on all the pattern pieces.

5. Pin Pattern's Top and Backing Layers

Align each top-layer pattern piece on each corresponding backing-layer piece, with both fabrics facing right side up, and pat the layers into place so that their edges are aligned. Securely pin together the edges of both layers on each piece.

6. Stitch Angie's Fall Pattern

Begin by inserting your needle $\frac{1}{8}$" inside the edge of one of the stenciled shapes on the top layer (your knot will show on the right side), and pull the thread through to the backing layer's wrong side. Then bring your needle back up to the right side of the top layer; using a straight stitch (see page 22), start sewing around the edge of each shape, $\frac{1}{8}$" inside that edge. When you arrive back at your starting point, knot off your thread on the right side of the pattern pieces.

Repeat the process to stitch around each stenciled shape. Continue stitching until you've outlined all the shapes with stitches.

7. Assemble Front and Back Pieces

With the fabrics' wrong sides together and the cut edges aligned, pin one Side Front piece to each side of the Center Front piece. Following the instructions for sewing floating seams on the right side on page 27 and using a straight stitch, begin sewing the pinned pieces together $\frac{1}{4}$" from the raw edges, starting at the top edge of the Camisole Dress. Wrap-stitch (see page 29) the beginning and end of every seam to secure it. As you sew, make sure to check your thread tension so the fabric lies flat before you tie off the thread at the end of your seam.

Repeat the process above to join the three pieces of the Camisole Dress's back, stitching one Side Back panel to each side of the Center Back panel.

8. Assemble Camisole Dress

With wrong sides together and the edges aligned, pin the shoulder seams of the Camisole Dress's completed front and back panels. Using a straight stitch, sew the shoulders together with a $\frac{1}{4}$" seam.

With wrong sides together and the edges aligned, pin and join the dress's side edges as you did the shoulder seams.

9. Bind Neckline and Armholes

Use the rotary cutter, cutting mat, and large plastic ruler to cut strips of leftover fabric $1\frac{1}{4}$" wide across the grain to use for binding the neckline and armholes. You'll need a total of about 80" of cut strips for the binding.

Use your iron to press each binding strip in half lengthwise, with wrong sides together, being careful not to stretch the fabric while pressing it. Starting at the dress's center-back neckline, encase the neckline's raw edge inside the folded binding, and pin the binding in place. When you need to add a new binding strip, simply overlap the strips' raw edges by about $\frac{1}{2}$" (or alternatively use the "Double U" method described in Step 7 of the String-Quilted Pillow on page 75). Finally overlap the binding's raw edges at the center back by about $\frac{1}{2}$", trimming any excess binding. Using the stretch stitch (see page 24) of your choice, sew through all layers and down the middle of the binding. Repeat the process to finish each armhole. Remove or simply break neckline and armhole basting stitches by pulling gently on one end of the thread. If some of the basting stitches are embedded in the binding, it's fine to leave them in place since the thread is broken and the stitches won't restrict the fabric's stretch.

Circle-Spiral Tunic

As I've grown older and found my own voice and style, I've come to recognize the beauty of both showing off the body and keeping parts hidden—and the importance of recognizing when each is appropriate. With this in mind, I intentionally made the back of this tunic, a variation of our bestselling Camisole Dress, long enough to reach past the top of the wearer's pants or skirt and, in the process, keep her underwear private. Like a mask at a costume ball, covering can be enthralling, sexy, and beautiful.

Our Design Choices

Top fabric — **Faded Black**

Backing fabric — **Faded Black**

Appliqué fabric — **Faded Leaves**

Binding fabric — **Faded Black**

Thread — **Black**

Stretch stitch — **Herringbone**

Seams — **Felled on wrong side**

Knots — **Inside garment**

Supplies

Camisole Tunic pattern (see pattern sheet at back of book)

4 yards of 60"-wide, cotton-jersey fabric, for tunic

¼ yard of 60"-wide, natural-color cotton-jersey fabric or a scrap measuring about 18" square, for appliqué

Supplies for Faded Leaves stenciling (see page 48)

Angie's Fall stencil (see page 31)

Paper scissors

Garment scissors

Rotary cutter and cutting mat

18" transparent plastic ruler

Tailor's chalk or disappearing-ink fabric pen

Hand-sewing needle

Button craft thread

All-purpose sewing thread

Pins

1. Color Appliqué Fabric with Faded Leaves

Following the instructions on page 48, wet-paint stencil in Faded Leaves color ¼ yard of natural-color cotton jersey (or a scrap measuring about 18" square) for the spiral appliqués that you'll cut and attach in steps 6 and 7. Allow the fabric to dry thoroughly.

2. Prepare and Cut Pattern

Photocopy or trace the Camisole Tunic pattern, and use your paper scissors to cut the photocopied or traced pattern in your desired size (see page 37), staying as close as possible to the black cutting lines. Note that the Center Front and Center Back pattern pieces are half-patterns, which are meant to be cut on folded fabric with the pattern edge marked "Place on fold" positioned accordingly. Note, too, that all the pattern pieces have a ¼" seam allowance built into the edges, except for the neckline, armhole, and hem edges, which, for this top, are left raw, with the neckline and armholes then bound.

This Camisole Tunic has a total of six pattern pieces: 1 Center Front, 2 Side Fronts, 1 Center Back, and 2 Side Backs.

You'll cut two fabric pieces for each pattern piece—a top layer and a backing layer—and you can cut these at the same time by layering two pieces of cotton jersey right side up. Make sure when positioning the two layers that the grain (see page 11) on each layer runs in the same direction. Likewise be sure to position the pattern piece on the two layers so that the fabrics' and pattern's grain lines run in the same direction.

Using tailor's chalk, trace around the pattern's edges. Then remove the pattern, and cut out the two pieces at once, using your rotary cutter and cutting mat, and making sure to cut in a smooth line just inside the chalked line so that you remove it entirely.

When finished, you'll have a total of 12 cut-fabric pattern pieces.

3. Baste Neck and Armholes

Using a single strand of all-purpose thread, baste (see page 22) all the neckline and armhole edges on the cut-fabric pieces, as indicated on the pattern pieces, to prevent these edges from stretching while you're working on your Camisole Tunic.

4. Align Top and Backing Layers

Place each top-layer pattern piece on each corresponding backing-layer piece, with the right sides of both fabrics facing up, and pat the layers into place so that their edges are aligned. Securely pin the edges of both layers together on each piece.

5. Assemble Front and Back Pieces

With the fabric right sides together and the cut edges aligned, pin a Side Front piece to each side of the Center Front piece. Following the instructions for sewing felled seams on the wrong side on page 28 and using a straight stitch (see page 22), begin stitching the pinned pieces together ¼" from the raw edges, starting at the top edge of the Camisole Tunic. Wrap-stitch (see page 29) the beginning and end of every seam to secure it. As you sew, make sure to check your thread tension so the fabric lies flat before you tie off the thread at the end of your seam.

Repeat the process above to join the three pieces of the Camisole Tunic's back, stitching one Side Back panel to each side of the Center Back panel.

6. Cut Circle Spiral Appliqués

Cut approximately 12 circle spirals (see page 51) from your Faded Leaves appliqué fabric in varying sizes from 5" to 7" in diameter. Your final placement of the appliqués will determine how many circle-spiral appliqués you actually need.

7. Place and Stitch Circle-Spiral Appliqués

Position and pin your cut circle-spiral appliqués on the constructed front and back of the Camisole Tunic. Stitch the appliqués in place according to the instructions on page 51.

8. Assemble Camisole Tunic

With right sides together and the cut edges aligned, pin the shoulder seams of the tunic's completed front and back center panels. Using a straight stitch, sew the shoulders together with a ¼" seam. As in Step 5, wrap-stitch the beginning and end of the seams to secure them, and check your thread tension as you sew.

With right sides together and the cut edges aligned, pin and join the tunic's side edges, as you did the shoulder seams.

9. Bind Neckline and Armholes

Follow the directions in Step 9 of the Inked & Quilted Camisole Dress on page 121 to bind the tunic's neckline and armholes.

String-Quilted & Stenciled Tank Top

A couple of years ago I covered a chair with a fabric we had used for one of our dresses. And with that small idea came the realization that we could create an entire home-furnishings line using the textiles we were already developing for our garments. Ultimately, we adopted a fluid design process, in which home furnishings and fashion all become inspiration for one another. This tank top is a good example of this type of crossover since it is made using the same techniques as the String-Quilted Pillow on page 73. The only difference is the shape of the pattern pieces and the colors.

Our Design Choices

Foundation fabric — **Natural**

String fabric — **White and natural**

Binding fabric — **Natural**

Stencil — **Angie's Fall**

Paint — **Light grey**

Thread — **Cream**

Stretch stitch — **Rosebud**

Seams — **Floating on wrong side**

Knots — **Inside garment**

Supplies

Tank Top pattern (see pattern sheet at back of book)

1 yard of 60"-wide cotton jersey for foundation

Cotton-jersey scraps at least 26" x 3", totaling about ¾ yard, for "string"

Angie's Fall stencil (see page 31)

Textile paint

Tools for your choice of stencil-transfer method (see page 42)

Paper scissors

Garment scissors

Rotary cutter and cutting mat

18" transparent plastic ruler

Tailor's chalk or disappearing-ink fabric pen

Hand-sewing needle

Button thread

All-purpose sewing thread

Pins

1. Prepare and Cut Pattern

Photocopy or trace the Tank Top pattern, and use your paper scissors to cut the photocopied or traced pattern in your desired size (see page 37), staying as close as possible to the black cutting lines. Note that the Center Front and Center Back pattern pieces are half-patterns, which are meant to be cut on folded fabric with the pattern edge marked "Place on fold" positioned accordingly. Note, too, that all the pattern pieces have a ¼" seam allowance built into the edges, except for the neckline, armhole, and hem edges, which, for this top, are left raw, with the neckline and armholes then bound.

This Tank Top has a total of six pattern pieces: 1 Center Front, 2 Side Fronts, 1 Center Back, and 2 Side Backs.

Lay out your cotton jersey foundation fabric right side up and make sure when positioning the pattern pieces on your fabric that the fabric's and pattern's grain lines (see page 11) run in the same direction. Using tailor's chalk, trace around the pattern's edges. Then remove the paper, and cut the fabric in a smooth line just inside the chalked line so that you remove it entirely.

When cutting the two Side Fronts and two Side Backs, you can layer two pieces of cotton jersey right side up and cut out both pieces at once. When aligning the two layers, make sure that the grain lines on both pieces of fabric and on the pattern all run in the same direction.

When finished, you will have a total of six cut-fabric foundation-pattern pieces.

2. Cut "String" and String-Quilt Pattern Pieces

Following the instructions for string-quilting on page 59, and using your prepared cotton-jersey scraps, string-quilt all the cut pattern pieces.

3. Baste Neck and Armholes

Using a single strand of all-purpose thread, baste (see page 22) all the neckline and armhole edges on the cut-fabric pieces, as indicated on the pattern pieces, to prevent these edges from stretching while you're working on your Tank Top.

4. Stencil Design on String-Quilted Pattern Pieces

Lay your string-quilted Tank Top's three front-pattern pieces right side up, placing each piece adjacent to its neighboring piece (see the illustration on page 120), so the stencil pattern will continue unbroken as you stencil the repeats. Place the Angie's Fall stencil on one of the two Side Front pieces. Using textile paint and the textile-paint-transfer method of your choice, carefully transfer the stencil design, and let the paint dry to the touch. Reposition the stencil to an adjacent area, and transfer the pattern again. Continue until you've stenciled an allover pattern on all three front-pattern pieces.

Repeat the process on the Tank Top's three back-pattern pieces, and allow all the stenciled designs to dry thoroughly.

5. Assemble Front and Back Pieces

With the fabrics' right sides together and the cut edges aligned, pin one Side Front piece to each side of the Center Front piece. Following the instructions for sewing floating seams on the wrong side on page 27 and using a straight stitch (see page 22), begin sewing the pinned pieces together ¼" from the raw edges, starting at the top edge of the Tank Top. Wrap-stitch (see page 29) the beginning and end of every seam to secure it. As you sew, make sure to check your thread tension so the fabric lies flat before you tie off the thread at the end of your seam.

Repeat the process above to join the three pieces of the Tunic Top's back, stitching one Side Back panel to each side of the Center Back panel.

6. Assemble Tank Top

With right sides together and the edges aligned, pin the shoulder seams of the Tank Top's completed front and back center panels. Using a straight stitch, sew the shoulders together with a ¼" seam.

With right sides together and the edges aligned, pin and join the side edges, as you did for the shoulder seams.

7. Bind Neckline and Armholes

Follow the directions in Step 9 of the Inked & Quilted Camisole Dress on page 121 to bind the tunic's neckline and armholes.

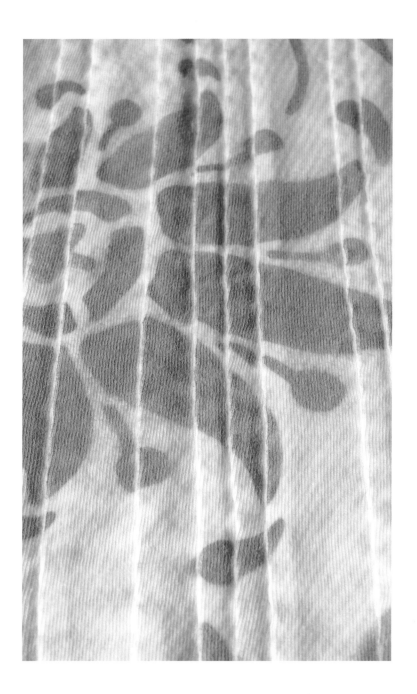

Dinner-on-the-Ground Table

This table is modeled after one we once borrowed from a church and used at a presentation in New York City. In the South, churches often set up tables like this one for their weekly Sunday lunches, which they call "dinner on the ground." Local ladies set out their delicacies on these long tables, then everyone fills a plate and sits down on quilts on the ground to eat. When the meal is finished, the tables are wiped down or hosed off and put away until next time.

We made our table with scrap wood, a choice you can make as well if you're willing to scrounge around your neighborhood and/or building sites. My partner, Butch, always says that you can build a house from what people throw away. We made our table about 14 feet long simply because the boards we found were that length. We nailed four 14'-long x 1" x 8" planks perpendicularly on top of seven 32"-long x 1" x 4" cross boards. Then, we placed our tabletop on four homemade sawhorses. (If you feel ambitious, you can make your own sawhorses, too. Or you may purchase sawhorse brackets with legs cut to your desired height at your local hardware store.) Last, we painted the table with VOC-free paint with an eggshell finish.

Alabama Studio Pickling Party

Although summer is a busy season, I always make time to spend a whole day with friends in the kitchen pickling food for the months ahead. Pickling is a bit of work, but it's so much fun to do with good friends, stories, music, and laughter. I usually prepare finger foods for these gatherings so that we have something delicious to eat as we go.

Menu

Slow-Roasted Squash

Pimiento Cheese

Chocolate Tartlets

The Pickling Recipes

Put-Up Tomatoes

Pickled Okra

John Kessler's Pickled Green Cherry Tomatoes

Slow-Roasted Squash
Serves 6–8

Crook-necked squash grow so prolifically in Alabama that I'm never surprised when I return home after a long day at work and find that one of my neighbors has left a big basket of it at my front door. This easy recipe is one of my family's favorite ways to enjoy the bounty.

All of the squash left on your porch (ideally young and tender with the flowers still attached to the ends)
Washed, freshly pulled green onions (as many as you can get)
Garlic cloves, sliced thinly
Extra-virgin olive oil
Salt and freshly ground black pepper
Cayenne pepper (optional)

Preheat oven to 300° F. Remove and discard the squash heads. If your squash are small (about 2" to 3" long), cut them in half lengthwise; if they are bigger, cut them into chunks about ½" to ¾" thick.

Place squash and whole green onions in a large bowl. Add the garlic and drizzle with olive oil. Add salt, pepper, and cayenne pepper (if using). Arrange single layered on a baking sheet and bake uncovered for 1½ to 2 hours, or until the squash pieces are soft and the green onions look slightly charred and caramelized.

Variation: I have baked both green and red tomatoes, whole garlic cloves, eggplant, zucchini, and bell peppers with my squash with great results. If you cut all of the vegetables about the same size, they should cook evenly. After baking, I sometimes garnish the veggies with shavings of Parmesan cheese and prosciutto from Benton's Smoky Mountain Country Hams.

Pimiento Cheese
Serves 6–8 - makes about 2½ cups

What can be said about pimiento cheese, except make it frequently and eat it often? I like it as a sandwich spread, on crackers, or troweled into celery stalks.

To make fresh pimientos, roast whole, washed red bell peppers from the garden in a 325° F. oven for about 20 minutes or until they have collapsed and started to turn black. When peppers are cool enough to handle, cut open, remove and discard seeds, peel away the skin, and dice. Do not wash the peppers after roasting as that will dilute their delicious flavor.

2½ cups grated sharp cheddar or hoop cheese
1 cup mayonnaise (storebought or homemade)
1 (7-ounce) jar of diced pimientos, drained, or ½ cup homemade
1 small sweet onion (or half a Vidalia onion since Vidalias tend to be large), minced with a knife or pulverized in a food processor almost to a liquid state
3–4 dashes Tabasco sauce
Salt and pepper to taste

In a large bowl, mix all of the ingredients together to form a thick paste. To make a sandwich spread, you may want to add a little extra mayonnaise. If possible, refrigerate overnight to give flavors time to marry.

Chocolate Tartlets
Makes twelve 3" tartlets

1 cup granulated sugar
⅓ cup all-purpose flour
1 cup buttermilk
2 large egg yolks, beaten
⅓ cup unsweetened cocoa
2 tablespoons unsalted butter
¼ teaspoon vanilla
Twelve 3" prebaked tartlet shells (see page 89)

Meringue

2 large egg whites
¼ teaspoon cream of tartar
¼ cup granulated sugar
¼ teaspoon vanilla

In the top of a double boiler, combine 1 cup sugar and the flour. Add buttermilk and simmer over boiling water for about 15 minutes, until thick. Remove from heat. Beat the egg yolks, and add them to the milk mixture. In a separate bowl, mix cocoa with enough boiling water to form paste, and whisk this paste into mixture in double boiler. Return to heat and simmer over boiling water until thick. Remove from heat, and add butter and ¼ teaspoon vanilla. Cool, then transfer to baked pastry tartlet shells.

While filling is cooling, preheat oven to 325° F, and prepare meringue as follows: In a medium-sized bowl, beat the egg whites and cream of tartar until mixture stands in a peak. Beat in ¼ cup sugar, 1 tablespoon at a time, and continue beating until stiff and glossy. Gently fold in ¼ teaspoon vanilla. Spread on top of prepared tartlets and bake until lightly browned, about 5 to 10 minutes.

Put-Up Tomatoes
Makes approximately 7 quarts

There is nothing like a homegrown tomato. In the South, you can fill a dinner conversation with stories of how to grow and process them, and the lengths to which people will go to get a good one. I eat them straight from the garden—like apples—make salads with them, and "put them up" (skins and all) for use year-round. Use this recipe for Put-Up Tomato Tart (see page 89), Alabama's Bloody Mary (see page 88), and for tomato sauces and purées.

21 pounds ripe tomatoes from garden (any kind will work)
Salt and freshly ground black pepper to taste
Water-bath canner and 7 quart-sized sterilized canning jars

Remove and discard stems from tomatoes. Cut tomatoes in half with skins over a stockpot, capturing the juice from the tomatoes as you cut. Drop tomato halves in pot. Season with salt and pepper. Cook tomatoes over medium heat for about 20 minutes or until they begin to soften just slightly. Do not add water; the juice from the ripe tomatoes is liquid enough.

Pour the cooked tomatoes into sterilized jars, and process in a water-bath canner for about 45 minutes, carefully following the instructions supplied with your canner. Remove jars from water bath, leave them to cool undisturbed, and store them at room temperature.

Pickled Okra
Makes 7–8 pints

3½ pounds small okra pods, washed
8 cloves garlic, peeled
8 small hot peppers
2 cups vinegar
⅓ cup pickling salt
2 teaspoons dill seeds
Water-bath canner and 8 pint-sized sterilized canning jars

Pack the okra tightly into hot, sterilized jars, leaving a bit of space at the top of the jar. Place 1 garlic clove and 1 hot pepper in each jar.

In a large saucepan, combine 1 quart water and the vinegar, pickling salt, and dill, and bring to a boil. Carefully pour the boiling mixture over the okra, leaving about ¼" headspace. Wipe the jar rims and seal immediately. Carefully following the instructions for your water-bath canner, process the jars in a boiling water bath for 10 minutes. Remove jars from water bath, leave them to cool undisturbed, and store them at room temperature.

John Kessler's Pickled Green Cherry Tomatoes (or "Tomolives")
Makes 1 quart

Atlanta Journal Constitution writer John Kessler offered us this pickled green tomato recipe as we walked through his bountiful backyard garden. These are excellent served as a party snack (like olives), as a condiment, or in a cocktail.

1 quart green cherry tomatoes (or quartered large green tomatoes)

½ bunch (6–8 stems) fresh dill

1 or 2 hot peppers, such as serrano or (if you are brave) habañero, sliced in half (optional)

½ cup cider vinegar

2 teaspoons salt

1 teaspoon freshly cracked black pepper

5 large cloves garlic, peeled and thickly sliced

1-quart sterilized canning jar

Note: Because the jar is not vacuum-sealed using a heating method, it must be kept in the refrigerator.

Stem the tomatoes; if using cherry tomatoes, pierce each one with a toothpick or skewer at the stem end, which allows the vinegar and spices to penetrate and flavor the flesh. Place the tomatoes in the 1-quart jar. Top with the whole dill sprigs and hot pepper (if using).

Bring 1½ cups water, the vinegar, salt, pepper, and garlic to a boil. Pour the hot liquid over the tomatoes to submerge. Stir the dill and garlic pieces into the jar. Cover and let come to room temperature. Store overnight in the refrigerator before serving.

Canning-Jar Covers

When canning during the summer, I always prepare more than my family can use so that I have extra to give away during the winter when the taste of summer is particularly sublime. For a special touch, I adorn each jar with a cotton-jersey cover.

To make these covers, cut either 10" or 7½" squares of cotton jersey and tie them around the tops of the jars with cotton-jersey pulls (see page 99). Sometimes I embellish my covers with a stencil design or one drawn with a black Sharpie marker.

Eyelet Doily

Doilies, like placemats, are a standard fixture in just about all Southern homes; you will find them made of every material known to mankind, from vinyl to tatted cotton. They seem to propagate in forgotten boxes at antique stores and thrift shops—and in a chest in my attic. This project takes the old-fashioned doily to a more modern place. It can be used for everything from lining your cake plate (see page 142) to protecting the table under a Bloody Mary bar (see page 88).

Our Design Choices

Base fabric — **White**

Backing fabric — **White**

Thread — **White**

Embroidery floss — **Cream and light grey**

Knots — **On wrong side**

Finished Size: 12" diameter (not including petals)

Supplies

Pattern paper (see page 14): one 11½" circle drawn on a 12" square, for doily center (use compass or dinner plate as guide); one 2" x 3" rectangle, for doily petals

1 yard of 60"-wide cotton jersey

Paper scissors

Garment scissors

Embroidery scissors

Rotary cutter and cutting mat

Tailor's chalk or disappearing-ink fabric pen

Hand-sewing needle

Button craft thread

Embroidery floss in two colors

Pins

1. Label Patterns

In the circle drawn on the pattern-paper square, draw a straight line parallel to one side of the square, and label this line "Grain Line" and the entire pattern piece "Doily Center."

For the Doily Petal pattern, trace the pattern at right on the 2" x 3" rectangle of pattern paper, and draw a straight line down the center of the pattern parallel to one long side of the rectangle. Label this line "Grain Line" and the entire pattern piece "Doily Petal," and cut out the pattern with your paper scissors.

2. Cut Out Doily Center and Petals

Each doily center is made from two layers of cotton jersey. To cut the two pieces needed for your doily center, layer and align two pieces of cotton jersey right side up. Make sure that the grain line (see page 11) on each layer runs in the same direction. Then position your Doily Center pattern on the two fabric layers so that fabrics' and pattern's grain lines likewise run in the same direction.

Using tailor's chalk, trace around the pattern's edges. Then remove the pattern, and cut out two pieces at once, using your rotary cutter and cutting mat, and making sure to cut in a smooth line just inside the chalked line so that you remove it entirely. You now have two doily centers.

Each of your 18 doily petals is also made from two layers of fabric. Using your Doily Petal pattern, repeat the cutting process above to cut a total of 36 doily petals.

3. Pin Doily Petals Together and Sew Edges

Align each doily petal's top and backing layers, right sides up, and pin the two layers together. Using a straight stitch (see page 22), begin stitching the pinned pieces together ¼" from the raw edges, starting at the top straight edge of the doily petal and stitching around the curve (you do not need to stitch across straight edge).

Doily Petal Pattern

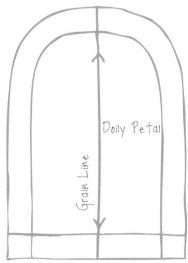

Wrap-stitch (see page 29) the beginning and end of the seam to secure it. As you sew, make sure to check your thread tension so the fabric lies flat before you tie off the thread at the end of your seam. Repeat process for remaining 17 doily petals.

4. Add Eyelet Embroidery to Doily Petals

Using two strands of embroidery floss doubled (to make four strands) and following the instructions on page 62, add eyelet embroidery to each of the 18 doily petals.

5. Construct Doily

Lay the bottom doily center right side down; then position and pin the 18 doily petals around the circumference of the bottom circle, overlapping its edge by ½". Lay the top doily center, right side up, over the bottom doily center, and pin it in place, repinning the petals as you pin the top so that all pins are on the top layer. Using a straight stitch, begin stitching around the circumference of the doily, ¼" from the raw edges (see the illustration below). As you sew, make sure to check your thread tension, so the fabric lies flat before you tie off at the end of your seam. Stitch around the entire circumference, securing each petal between the two layers of the center.

Pin and Sew Doily Pieces

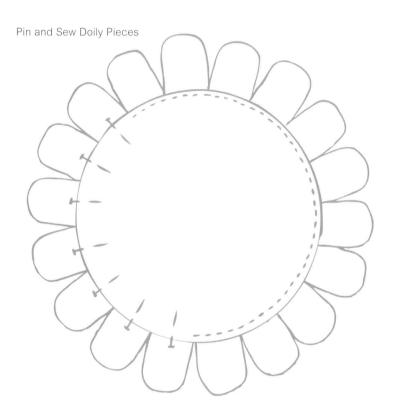

6. Add Eyelet Embroidery to Doily Center
After constructing your doily, use two strands of embroidery floss doubled and add eyelet embroidery to the doily center. Add as much or little embroidery as you like.

Homemade Cake Plate

Whenever I go thrifting, it's the old, printed glasses and lonely plates that I'm drawn to, and my kitchen and china cabinets are filled with stacks of strays that I've picked up all over the world as well as odds and ends I've inherited. This simple cake plate is the perfect project for these "castaways," as my family calls them. Because the hardest part of this project is drilling the holes in the plates, glass, and bowl, I have my holes drilled professionally at a local glass store. Any shop selling glass is set up for drilling it (and china) but will warn you that glass and porcelain may break when drilled. To this day, I have never had a single piece crack or break. But, to be safe, I always supply double what I really need, and I never give them anything I would be very sad to lose. That way the person doing the drilling feels secure.

This simple cake plate calls for two plates, one glass, and one small bowl. Holes are drilled through the center of each and then a ¼" threaded rod is inserted to hold the whole thing together with two ¼" washers, one ¼" standard nut, and one ¼" acorn nut.

After your holes are drilled, stack your pieces on your work surface with the holes lined up and insert your threaded rod. Letting the rod rest on the work surface, measure ⅛" from the top plate up the length of the threaded rod, and mark this spot with a Sharpie marker. Using a hand saw, cut the threaded rod to your desired length. To finish, add washers and nuts to each end of the threaded rod. I use my acorn nut for the top of my cake plate and adjust the bottom nut to hold all of the dishes securely in place. Take care not to tighten your nut too much, as it can cause the porcelain to crack over time.

I keep one of my cake plates on my dressing table to hold jewelry and use another one to serve desserts, sometimes with a paper doily or with the Eyelet Doily on page 139.

Small Medallion Placemats

These placemats are a variation of the Eyelet-Embroidered Placemats on page 83. Use the instructions there to make matching napkins. We used these Small Medallion Placemats for our Celebration dinner on page 112, placing them all in a line in the center of the table like a runner.

Our Design Choices

Base fabric — **Red**

Backing fabric — **Red**

Stencil — **Small Medallion**

Textile paint — **Burgundy**

Embroidery floss — **Red**

Knots — **On wrong side**

Finished Size: 14" x 20"

Supplies

Pattern paper (see page 14): one 14" x 20" piece

4 yards of 60"-wide cotton jersey, for 6 placemats (plus 2 yards more for napkins; see page 83)

Small Medallion stencil (see pullout after page 144)

Textile paint

Tools for your choice of stencil-transfer method (see page 42)

Garment scissors

Embroidery scissors

Rotary cutter and cutting mat

18" transparent plastic ruler

Tailor's chalk or disappearing-ink fabric pen

Hand-sewing needle

Embroidery floss

Pins

1. Label Pattern

On the pattern paper, draw a straight line parallel to the rectangle's short sides, and label this line "Grain Line" and the entire pattern piece "Placemat."

Labeling Pattern

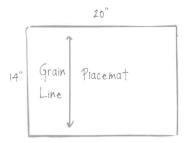

2. Cut Out Placemats

Each placemat is made from three layers of cotton jersey and you can cut them out two pieces at a time. Make sure when positioning the two layers that the grain line (see page 11) on each layer runs in the same direction. Then position your Placemat pattern piece on the two fabric layers so that the fabrics' and pattern's grain lines likewise run in the same direction.

Using tailor's chalk, trace around the pattern's edges. Then remove the pattern and cut out two pieces at once, using your rotary cutter and cutting mat, and making sure to cut in a smooth line just inside the chalked line so that you remove it entirely. You now have two placemat pieces. Repeat the cutting process until you have a total of 18 pieces for six placemats.

3. Stencil Design on Pattern Pieces

Lay the placemat's top layer right side up on your work area (see page 42) and place the Small Medallion stencil on top of it at one short end. Using textile paint and the stencil-transfer method of your choice, carefully transfer the stencil design onto the pattern piece, and let the paint dry to the touch. Then reposition the stencil at the opposite end of the placemat, and repeat the transfer process. Let the stenciled designs dry thoroughly.

4. Pin Placemats Together and Backstitch Medallion Stencil

Align the placemat's top and two backing layers, right sides up, and pin the layers together.

Backstitch (see page 23) around the edge of each element of the stenciled design on the placemat's top layer, sewing through all three layers of the placemat.

5. Sew Long Edges Together

Backstitch the pinned pieces together ¼" from the raw edges on one long side, starting at the top edge of the backstitched Small Medallion design and sewing across to the backstitched design on the other end. As you sew, make sure to check your thread tension so the fabric lies flat before you tie off the thread at the end of your seam. Repeat the above process on the placemat's other long side.

Alabama Studio Apron

I spend a lot of time in the kitchen, which means I also spend a lot of time in an apron. I keep a ready stack of homemade ones on hand for myself and for guests who want to help cook.

To make one, cut a 36" square of cotton jersey. Leave as is or add a pocket or embellish with a stencil and/or decorative stitching or writing. Tie around the waist using a cotton-jersey pull (see page 99). To make this apron for a child, cut an 18" square of cotton jersey and tie just under the arms.

Once an apron becomes soiled, I cut it into four 18" squares and use them as rags. Alternatively, you could just start with 18" squares and use them as napkins or rags.

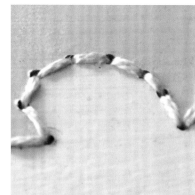

Stenciled & Sewn Table

I love revamping furniture that has seen better days, which means that all sorts of wardrobes, cabinets, and tables in various stages of repair—and disrepair—fill our house, barn, and back patio. My partner is notorious for picking up lonely pieces left by the roadside. When he found the table shown here, it was bright orange and had a loose leg. We fixed the leg, painted the table white, decorated it with a stencil motif, then finally drilled holes around portions of the stenciled motif and stitched through the holes with twine.

Our Design Choices

Base paint — **VOC-free white in eggshell finish**

Stencil paint — **VOC-free tan in eggshell finish**

Twine — **Cream**

Stencil — **Large Medallion**

Supplies

1 coffee table

1 gallon VOC-free paint (that is, without volatile organic chemicals), for base

1 quart VOC-free paint, for stenciling

1 paintbrush

Large Medallion stencil (see page 66)

Tools for your choice of stencil-transfer method (see page 42)

Pencil

Electric drill with $\frac{1}{8}$" drill bit

Large embroidery needle

Twine, thread, or string

1. Paint Your Table

Paint your table white and let it dry. Apply as many coats as you like.

2. Stencil Design on Tabletop

Place the Large Medallion stencil on your tabletop. Using your stencil paint and the stencil-transfer method of your choice (see page 42), carefully transfer the stencil design to the top of the table, and let the paint dry to the touch. Then reposition the stencil, and repeat the transfer process as needed to fill the entire tabletop.

3. Drill Holes

First select the elements of your stenciled design on your tabletop that you want to highlight with stitching (we picked three), making sure that none of these elements crosses the table's supports (sewing an element positioned over a cross support requires drilling though both the table and cross support—a slightly tricky, awkward maneuver that's best avoided). Next mark drill holes, using a pencil to make small dots $\frac{1}{4}$" apart around each area you're going to outline with stitches.

Prepare your drill, and then drill the marked holes. Drilling through the wood can be time-consuming and, for me, requires a lot of patience.

4. Sew Table

Thread a needle with twine, thread, or string (each produces a slightly different effect. Knot off (see page 21), tying a large knot. Begin by inserting your needle through one drilled hole of one stenciled shape from bottom of table, pull the thread through to top of table, stitch into the neighboring hole, and bring your needle back down to bottom side of table. Next, using a backstitch (see page 23), start sewing around the edge of the shape through the drilled holes. When you arrive back at starting point, knot off thread on wrong side of table.

Knot your thread again, move to next stenciled shape, and repeat the stitching process. Continue stitching around each shape in stenciled design until all are outlined.

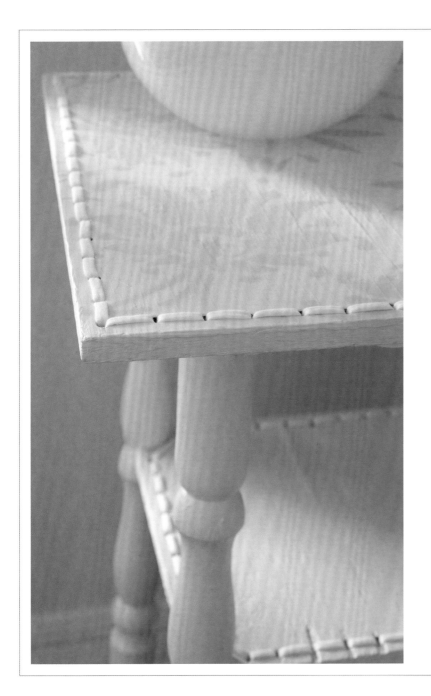

Stitching Furniture

I hope the Stenciled & Sewn Table will inspire you to explore other ways to embellish furniture with stitchwork. At Alabama Chanin we have appliquéd cotton jersey scraps to the wire-screen fronts of a pie safe, appliquéd wood cut into stencil shapes onto a set of dresser drawers, and drilled around an existing pattern on a piece of wood and backstitched through the holes with twine.

For the side table shown here, which sits in my entryway, I drilled holes ½" from the outside edge of the tabletop and then painted the entire table with VOC-free white paint, stenciled Angie's Fall on the tabletop in beige, and finally, sewed through the drilled holes with ½"-wide cotton-jersey pulls cut from white scraps (see page 99).

Relief Appliqué Chair Pillow

I started making these comfy chair pillows to add some extra padding to our woven chair seats but since then have used them for many other purposes, both utilitarian and aesthetic. Compact and easy, this is a great project to work on during road trips or waiting periods at doctors' offices.

Our Design Choices

Pillow fabric — **Natural**

Appliqué fabric — **White**

Piping fabric — **White**

Embroidery floss — **Cream**

Stencil — **Angie's Fall**

Paint — **White**

Thread — **Cream**

Knots — **Inside pillow**

Finished Size: 12" x 14"

Supplies

One 12½" x 14½" rectangle and one 12½" x 9" rectangle of pattern paper or butcher paper (see page 14)

¾ yard of 60"-wide cotton jersey in one color

¼ yard of 60"-wide cotton jersey in second color, for appliqué, plus enough cotton-jersey scraps in second color to make 80" of ½"-wide piping

Angie's Fall stencil (see page 31)

Textile paint

Tools for your choice of stencil-transfer method (see page 42)

Garment scissors

Embroidery scissors

Rotary cutter and cutting mat

18" transparent plastic ruler

Tailor's chalk or disappearing-ink fabric pen

Hand-sewing needle

Button craft thread

Pins

12" x 14" pillow form

1. Label Patterns

On the 12½" x 14½" rectangle of pattern or butcher paper, draw a line parallel to the short side. Label the line "Grain Line" and the rectangle itself "Relief Appliqué Pillow Front."

On the 12½" x 9" rectangle of pattern paper, draw a line parallel to the long side. Label it "Grain Line" and the rectangle itself "Relief Appliqué Pillow Back."

Labeling Patterns

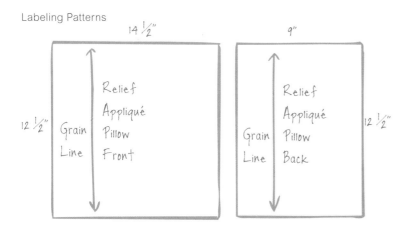

2. Cut Out Pillow Front and Back

Cut your ½ yard of fabric in half widthwise, and layer the two pieces right side up, making sure that the grain line (see page 11) on both pieces runs in the same direction. Place the Relief Appliqué Pillow Back pattern on top of the two aligned layers, again matching the direction of the pattern's marked grain line with the fabrics' grain lines.

Using tailor's chalk, trace around the pattern's edges. Then remove the pattern, and cut out two pieces at once, using your rotary cutter and cutting mat, and making sure to cut in a smooth line just inside the chalked line so that you remove it entirely. You now have two pillow-back pieces.

Reposition your pattern piece, and repeat the process so that you have a total of four pillow-back pieces.

Repeat the process above using the Relief Appliqué Pillow Front pattern and cutting a total of two front pieces.

When finished, you'll have four fabric Relief Appliqué Pillow Backs and two fabric Relief Appliqué Pillow Fronts in the same color.

3. Stencil Design on Pillow Front

Lay the cut pattern piece for the pillow-front's top layer right side up, and place Angie's Fall stencil on top of it. Using textile paint and the stencil-transfer method of your choice (see page 42), carefully transfer the stencil design onto the pattern piece, and let the paint dry to the touch. To cover the fabric entirely with the stenciled image, reposition the stencil as needed, and transfer the design again, allowing the paint to dry to the touch between each repositioning. Then allow the stenciled designs to dry thoroughly.

4. Stencil Design on Appliqué Fabric

The stencil for your appliqué fabric needs to be a 15-percent enlargement (see page 53) of the Angie's Fall stencil used in Step 3. You can enlarge the stencil image at any copy shop, and then follow the directions on page 39 to create the actual stencil.

Lay your appliqué fabric wrong side up. Turn your enlarged Angie's Fall stencil to the wrong side, and position it on the appliqué fabric. By stenciling the wrong side of your fabric, the finished appliqué pieces will not show any markings from the stencil-transfer paint or marker. Using textile paint and the stencil-transfer method of your choice, carefully transfer the enlarged stencil design onto the fabric, and let the stenciled design dry thoroughly. Repeat the stencil-transfer process, as needed, to make enough appliqué fabric for your stenciled pillow top. Cut out the transferred stencil's medium and large individual petals and leaves, carefully cutting around the edge of each stenciled shape. Because the small shapes in the design will be too difficult to appliqué, don't worry about cutting them out. Instead you'll backstitch around these small shapes on the pillow front's transferred design in Step 6.

5. Relief Appliqué Medium and Large Shapes

Using your stenciled appliqués from Step 4, follow the instructions for relief appliqué on page 53 to appliqué each medium and large shape of the stenciled design on the pillow front.

6. Backstitch Small Shapes

Backstitch (see page 23) around each of the remaining small shapes in the stenciled design on the pillow front.

7. Prepare and Pin Piping to Pillow Front

To cut, prepare, and pin piping strips on the follow front, follow the directions in Step 7 of the String-Quilted Pillow on page 75.

8. Pin and Stitch Front to Backs

To construct your pillow, follow the directions in Step 8 of the String-Quilted Pillow. Then turn your pillowcase right side out, and slip your pillow into the case.

Small Medallion Pillow

To make this simple variation of the Relief Appliqué Chair Pillow, for Step 3, we used butcher paper to mask off all but a 2"-wide strip of our top fabric down the right-hand side. We then placed the Small Medallion stencil (see pullout after page 144) over this 2"-wide strip and on top of the butcher paper, and spray-painted the stenciled area with textile paint. Finally we backstitched around all of the shapes in the stencil design with embroidery floss. Masking is a great way to get varying effects out of a single stencil.

Spiral Appliqué & Beaded Camisole Dress

When I design, I always think about what a piece will look like from a distance and up close. I love the idea of luring people in as they get closer and closer. The experience of viewing this dress, for example, begins with the two tones of the circle-spiral appliqués. As you move closer, you begin to notice the stitching, then the beautifully stenciled Faded Leaves color effect, and finally the beads. Of course, all of this lovely detail is time-consuming to create, but it also makes for an heirloom piece that can be enjoyed for generations.

Our Design Choices

Top fabric — **Moss green**

Backing fabric — **Moss green**

Binding fabric — **Moss green**

Appliqué fabric — **Faded Leaves and light pink**

Thread — **Grey for Faded Leaves and appliqué**
Pink for pink appliqué
Light green for dress construction

Stretch stitch — **Rosebud**

Seams — **Felled on wrong side**

Knots — **Inside garment**

Beads — **Pink bugle beads**
Pink chop beads

Supplies

Camisole Dress pattern (see pattern sheet at back of book)

6 yards of 60"-wide cotton-jersey fabric

¼ yard of 60"-wide natural cotton-jersey fabric, for circle appliqué

Supplies for Faded Leaves stenciling (see page 48)

¼ yard of 60"-wide cotton-jersey fabric, for second color of circle appliqué

Angie's Fall stencil (see page 31)

Paper scissors

Garment scissors

Rotary cutter and cutting mat

18" transparent plastic ruler

Tailor's chalk or disappearing-ink fabric pen

Hand-sewing needle

Button craft thread

All-purpose sewing thread

Pins

650 bugle beads and 2,880 chop beads

1. Color Appliqué Fabric with Faded Leaves

Following the instructions on page 48, wet-paint-stencil ¼ yard of natural cotton jersey for the 52 spiral appliqués that you'll cut and attach in steps 6 and 7.

2. Prepare and Cut Pattern

Photocopy or trace the Camisole Dress pattern, and use your paper scissors to cut the photocopied or traced pattern in your desired size (see page 37), staying as close as possible to the black cutting lines. Note that the Center Front and Center Back pattern pieces are half-patterns, which are meant to be cut on folded fabric with the pattern edge marked "Place on fold" positioned accordingly. Note, too, that all the pattern pieces have a ¼" seam allowance built into the edges, except for the neckline, armhole, and hem edges, which, for this dress, are left raw and then bound.

The Camisole Dress has a total of six pattern pieces: 1 Center Front, 2 Side Fronts, 1 Center Back, and 2 Side Backs.

You'll cut two fabric pieces for each pattern piece—a top layer and a backing layer—and you can cut these two pieces at the same time by layering two pieces of the cotton jersey right side up. Make sure when positioning the two layers that the grain line (see page 11) on each layer runs in the same direction. Likewise be sure to position the pattern piece on the two layers so that the fabrics' and pattern's grain lines run in the same direction.

Using tailor's chalk, trace around the pattern's edges. Then remove the pattern and cut out the two pieces at once, using your rotary cutter and cutting mat, and making sure to cut in a smooth line just inside the chalked line to remove it entirely.

When finished, you'll have a total of 12 cut-fabric pattern pieces.

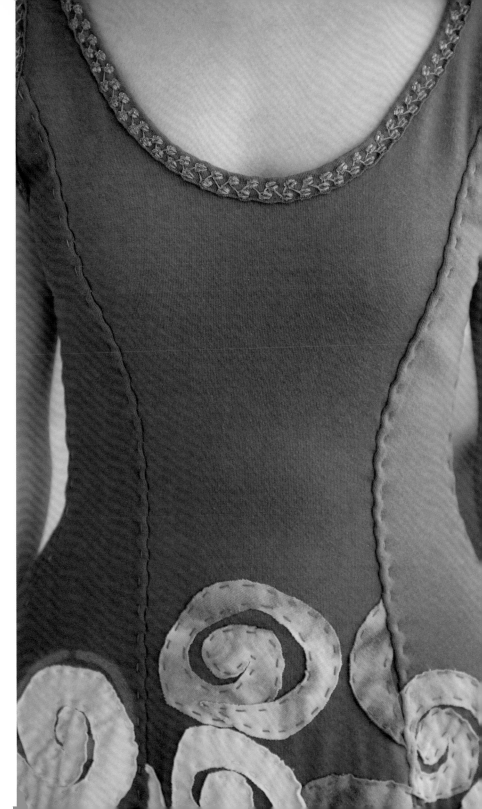

3. Baste Neck and Armholes

Using a single strand of all-purpose thread, baste (see page 22) all the neckline and armhole edges on the cut pattern pieces, as labeled on the pattern pieces, to prevent these edges from stretching while you're working on your Camisole Dress.

4. Pin Pattern's Top and Backing Layers

Align each top-layer pattern piece on each corresponding backing-layer piece, with both fabrics facing right side up; and pat the layers into place so that their edges are aligned. Securely pin the edges of both layers together.

5. Assemble Front and Back Pieces

With the fabric right sides together and the cut edges aligned, pin one Side Front piece to each side of the Center Front piece. Following the instructions for sewing felled seams on the wrong side on page 28 and using a straight stitch (see page 22), begin stitching the pinned pieces together ¼" from the raw edges, starting at the top edge of the Camisole Dress. Wrap-stitch (see page 29) the beginning and end of every seam to secure it. As you sew, make sure to check your thread tension so the fabric lies flat before you tie off the thread at the end of your seam.

Repeat the process above to join the three pieces of the Camisole Dress's back, stitching the one Side-Back panel to each side of the Center Back panel.

6. Cut Circle-Spiral Appliqué

Cut approximately 52 circle spirals (see page 51) from your Faded Leaves appliqué fabric in varying sizes from 4" to 8" in diameter. Then cut approximately 23 circle spirals in similar varying diameters from your pink appliqué fabric. Your final placement will determine how many circle spiral appliqués you actually use.

7. Stitch Circle-Spiral Appliqués in Place

Place your cut circle-spiral appliqués on the constructed front and back of your dress, and pin them in place. Following the instructions on page 51, stitch your appliqués to the dress.

8. Bead Front and Back Panels

Following the instructions for cluster beading on page 64, add beads to your front and back panels using the detail photo on page 156 for inspiration. Note that you should avoid beading in the ¼" seam allowance on each side of your front and back panels since the beads will make construction in the next step more difficult.

9. Assemble Camisole Dress

With right sides together and the cut edges aligned, pin the shoulder seams of the Camisole Dress's completed front and back panels. Sew the shoulder seams, wrap-stitching the edges and checking your tension as you sew.

With right sides together, pin and join the dress's side seams as you did the shoulder seams.

10. Bind Neckline, Armholes, and Hem of Dress

Follow the directions in Step 9 of the Inked & Quilted Camisole Dress on page 121 to prepare and pin the binding in place on the dress's neckline and armholes. Then, using the beaded stretch stitch of your choice (see beaded rosebud or beaded whipstitch, page 65), sew through all layers and down the middle of the neckline binding to attach and finish it.

Next attach and finish the armhole binding using the stretch stitch but no beads, which would be uncomfortable under the arm with extended wear.

Finally repeat the binding process using a beaded stretch stitch to bind the dress's hem.

   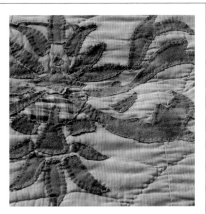

Textile Stories

"Much of the social history of early America has been lost to us precisely because women were expected to use needles rather than pens. Yet if textiles are in one sense an emblem of women's oppression, they have also been an almost universal medium of female expression. If historians are to understand the lives of women in times past, they must not only cherish the Anne Bradstreets and Martha Ballards who mastered the mysterious ways of quill pens, they must also decipher work composed in yarn and thread."

—Pulitzer Prize-winning historian Laurel Thatcher Ulrich

Over the past decade or so I have recorded many oral histories from quilters and textile workers all over Alabama. When I first started collecting these stories, I imagined they would eventually become part of a larger archive. But it occurred to me one afternoon that these oral histories tell a patchwork story in the same way that the old quilts I collect tell stories.

And in that moment, I understood that the stories of these people need to be embroidered into quilts to fully complete the cycle.

Many of the quilts I collect are what people around here call "garbage quilts," that is, quilts that are so far beyond repair that they are no longer considered presentable. Most people use these quilts as blankets for barn animals or to move furniture, but today, we stabilize "garbage quilts"—making no effort at restoration, which would be impossible—then hand-embroider them with stories from my oral histories so both will endure for posterity.

We have proudly displayed these quilts at galleries, museums, and stores around the world. If you have access to old quilts from your family, community, or region, you can easily replicate this process, embroidering the quilts with stories you want to keep and share.

Angie's Fall Design Variations

I have been working with stencils since the very beginning of this adventure that has become Alabama Chanin. From the first letter stencils purchased at the hardware store to use to embellish T-shirts to the elaborate floras we have developed more recently, stencils have been an integral part of all of our collections.

The Angie's Fall stencil is a favorite of mine. It is named after my friend Angie Mosier, who developed the recipes for this book, and for the season—Fall 2008—in which we first used it. At that time I was striving to find a way to move from one collection to the next organically rather than by coming up with an idea, using it for one season, and then replacing it with something else (a typical cycle in the fashion industry). With Angie's Fall, I realized I could introduce an idea one season and also give it more time to grow and reach its full maturity in another. And so another version of Angie's Fall appeared in our Fall 2009 collection. This philosophy of continual development is at the core of the Slow Food Movement, a movement I came to understand with Angie's help, thus the nod to her in the name of this stencil.

On the pages that follow are three couture fabrics designed with the Angie's Fall stencil but embellished differently by mixing and matching techniques for which we have given instructions in this book. In the photographs opposite and on pages 170–173 you can see how the fabrics can be applied to a variety of projects. While you can, of course, replicate exactly what is shown here, I hope that you will be inspired by everything you have seen and learned in this book to mix and match stencils, colors, and techniques to create your own unique style.

Fabric 1 - Iced Angie

To create Iced Angie fabric: 1. Stencil fabric using Angie's Fall. 2. Using a Sharpie marker, trace large flower petals and small shapes around them. 3. Backstitch ¹/₈" inside edge of large traced flower petals.

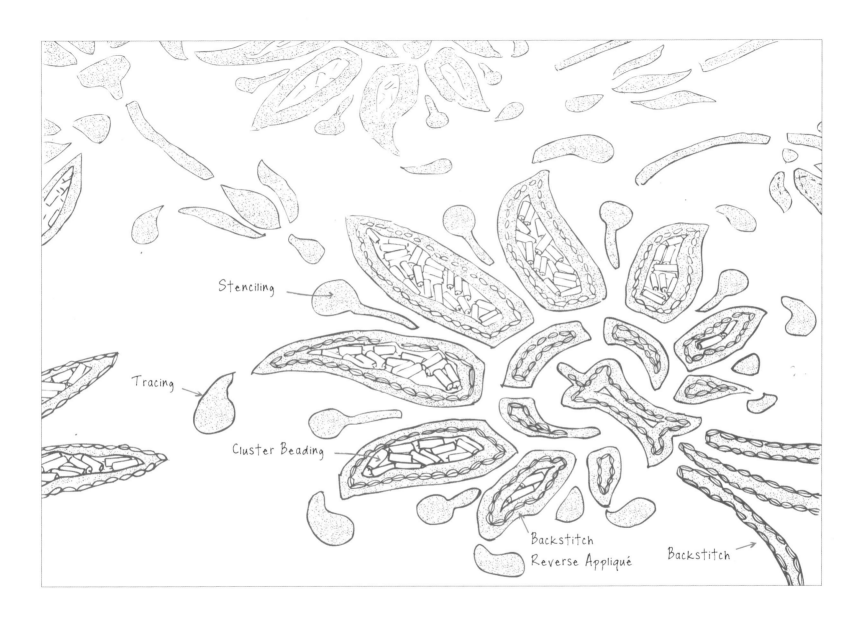

Stenciling

Tracing

Cluster Beading

Backstitch
Reverse Appliqué

Backstitch

4. Cut reverse appliqué inside large backstitched shapes. 5. Backstitch remaining stenciled shapes. 6. Add cluster beading inside cut reverse-appliqué petals.

Fabric 2 - Special Angie's Fall

To create Special Angie's Fall fabric: 1. Stencil fabric using Angie's Fall. 2. Add relief appliqué to large flower petals.

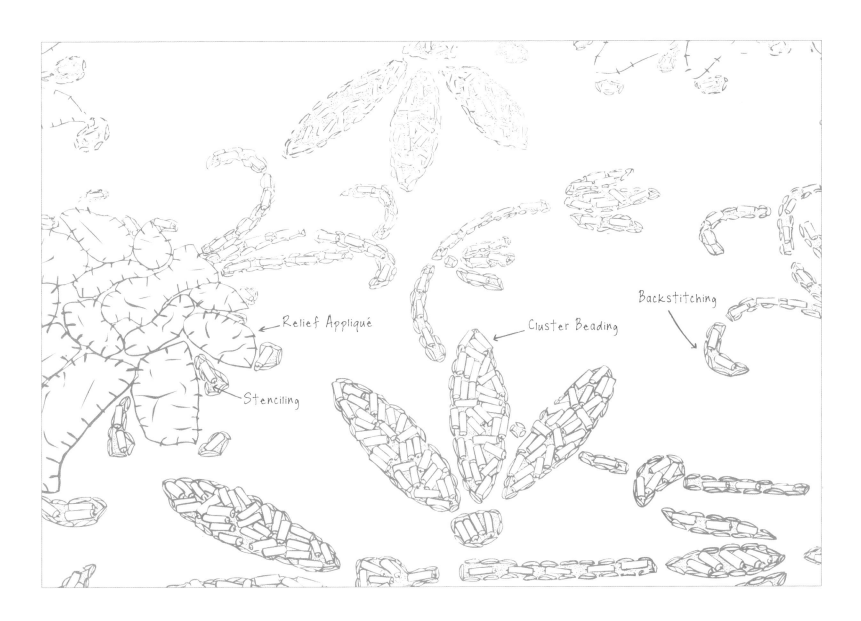

Relief Appliqué

Stenciling

Cluster Beading

Backstitching

3. Backstitch all remaining stenciled shapes. 4. Add cluster beading inside all backstitched stenciled shapes.

Fabric 3 – Eyelet & Angie

To create Eyelet & Angie fabric: 1. Stencil fabric using Angie's Fall. 2. Add relief appliqué to large flower petals.
3. Backstitch all remaining stenciled shapes, and cut out medium and large reverse-appliqué shapes, leaving very small shapes

Stenciling

Eyelets

Beaded Eyelet

Backstitch
Reverse Appliqué

Cluster Beading

Relief Appliqué

backstitched but uncut. 4. Add eyelets and beaded eyelets around all leaf and flower stenciled shapes. 5. Add cluster beading at base of backstitched reverse-appliqué petals.

Iced Angie Dining Room Chairs

I love upholstering furniture with our hand-sewn fabrics. I used Iced Angie fabric for these chairs because I wanted to introduce this darker blue color into my kitchen.

To create upholstery fabric for your own furniture, first show the furniture to an upholsterer and ask him or her how much fabric you will need. On a more complicated piece, the upholsterer can actually provide you with a pattern for each of the pieces. Next, cut out the fabric, apply the stencil, and stitch only the area that will be seen on the finished piece of furniture. Finally, take your fabric back to the upholsterer to apply to the furniture.

Special Angie's Fall Dress

I designed this variation of the Tank Dress with Relief Appliqué for our Fall 2009 Songbirds Collection. To make one of your own, follow the fabric instructions on page 166 and the Tank Dress instructions on page 79. I love the mixture of techniques and colors and especially the surprise of finding the pattern on the back of the dress as well as the front.

Eyelet & Angie Couch Saver

Couch savers were a permanent fixture in my grandmother's home. All manner of crocheted, quilted, and plain fabrics were safety-pinned to upholstered couch backs as well as the arms and heads of chairs in order to protect the fabric from undue wear and tear. In homage to Gramperkins, who taught me just about everything I love about domesticity, I created this couch saver. To make one of your own, cut a 36" x 48" piece of cotton jersey and embellish it as shown on page 168. Then, to finish, add blanket stitch around all four edges. I love to read, relax, and watch movies in bed rather than on my couch, so that is where I display and enjoy this beautiful work.

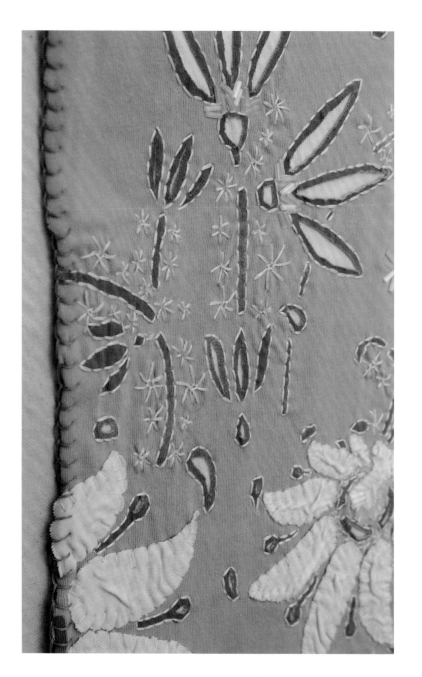

Acknowledgments

First and foremost, thank you to our readers and supporters. Without you, this work would not be possible.

Thank you to my entire family, especially my grandparents, Stanley & Lucille Perkins and Aaron & Christine Smith, who lived by the earth and taught me well. And to those who bring light to my life everyday: Billy Smith, Sherry Dean Smith, Butch Anthony, Maggie Anthony-Chanin, and Zach Chanin.

And to my work family: Steven Smith, Diane Hall, Jessica Turner, Chancey Praytor, Kay Woehle, Michelle Nichols, and our talented artisans—without all of you, this work would not exist.

And to our extended work family: Robert & Jennifer Rausch, Chris Timmons, Alli Coate, Sara Martin, Conrad Pitts, Terry Wiley, Eva Whitechapel, Marisa Keris, Sandi and Mareth McGee, Shawn Wallace, John Kessler, Jordyn and Bradley Dean, Elizabeth DeRamus, and a host of others who provide support, stories, and inspiration.

A big Southern hug to Angie Mosier who has taught me to live life with my plate full.

And most of all, thank you to Melanie Falick, our editor, for her constant belief, dedication, and diligence.

About the Author

Natalie Chanin, former costume designer and fashion stylist, is the founder and head designer of Alabama Chanin. Her work has been featured in *Vogue*, *Time*, the *New York Times*, and *Town & Country*, as well as on CBS news. She is the author of *Alabama Stitch Book* (STC, 2007). Natalie is a member of the Council of Fashion Designers of America, and her work was selected for the 2010 Global Triennial by the Cooper-Hewitt, National Design Museum. She works in her hometown of Florence, Alabama, as an entrepreneur, designer, writer, collector of stories, filmmaker, mother, gardener, and cook.

Most of the materials and tools called for in the projects in this book are available from fabric and craft retailers and from the Alabama Chanin website. Kits for many of the projects are also available on the website (www.alabamachanin.com).

Published in 2010 by Stewart, Tabori & Chang
An imprint of ABRAMS

Text copyright © 2010 by Natalie Chanin
Photographs copyright © 2010 by Robert Rausch
Illustrations copyright © 2010 by Alli Coate

Library of Congress Cataloging-in-Publication Data

Chanin, Natalie.
Alabama Studio Style / Natalie Chanin.
p. cm.
ISBN 978-1-58479-823-1
1. Handicraft. 2. Sustainable living. 3. Salvage (Waste, etc.) I. Title.
TT157.C367 2010
745.5--dc22
2009015800

Editor: **Melanie Falick**
Technical Editor: **Chris Timmons**
Designer: **Robert Rausch**
Production Manager: **Jacqueline Poirier**

The text of this book was composed in Arial and Palatino.

Printed and bound in China
10 9 8 7 6 5 4 3 2 1

ABRAMS
THE ART OF BOOKS SINCE 1949
115 West 18th Street
New York, NY 10011
www.abramsbooks.com